REAL MEN, REAL FAITH

FOREWORD BY RICK WARREN
COMPILED BY GENE WILLIAMS

Beacon Hill Press of Kansas City
Kansas City,

Copyright 2004
by Beacon Hill Press of Kansas City

ISBN 083-412-1352

Printed in the
United States of America

Cover Design: Ted Ferguson

10 9 8 7 6 5 4 3 2 1

CONTENTS

FOREWORD

Rick Warren

If there ever was a real man who had real faith, it was my dad. He spent his life believing in and trusting Jesus and making every conceivable effort to tell others about Him. He did not have an easy life, but he proved that he had found something worth living for and sharing with others.

My father was a minister for more than 50 years, serving mostly in small rural churches. He was a simple preacher, but he was a man with a mission. His favorite activity was taking teams of volunteers overseas to build church buildings for small congregations. In his lifetime Dad helped build more than 150 churches around the world.

In 1999 my father died of cancer. In the final week of his life, the disease kept him awake in a semiconscious state nearly 24 hours a day. As he dreamed, he would talk out loud about what he was dreaming. Sitting by his bedside, I learned a lot about my dad by just listening to his dreams. He relived one church building project after another.

One night near the end while my wife, my niece, and I were by his side, Dad suddenly became very active and tried to get out of bed. Of course, he was too weak, and my wife insisted that he lie back down. But he persisted in trying to get out of bed, so my wife finally asked, "Jimmy, what are you trying to do?"

He replied, "Got to save one more for Jesus! Got to save one more for Jesus! Got save one more for Jesus!"

During the next hour he said that phrase probably a hundred

times: "Got to save one more for Jesus!" As I sat by his bed with tears flowing down my cheeks, I bowed my head to thank God for my dad's faith. At that moment he reached out and placed his frail hand on my head and said, as if commissioning me, "Save one more for Jesus! Save one more for Jesus!"

I intend for that to be the theme of the rest of my life. I invite you to consider it as a focus for your life, too, because nothing will make a greater difference for eternity. If you want God to use you, you must care about what He cares about; what He cares about most is the redemption of the people He made. He wants His lost children found! Nothing matters more to God; the Cross proves that. I pray that you'll always be on the lookout to reach "one more for Jesus" so that when you stand before God one day, you can say, "Mission accomplished!"

It took a real man with real faith to live the life that the apostle Paul lived. He needed enormous physical stamina in order to undertake the journeys that he did. His words to the church at Thessalonica speak of him, my dad, hopefully me, and you: Your lives are echoing the Master's Word. "The news of your faith in God is out. We don't even have to say anything anymore—*you're* the message!" (1 Thess. 1:8, TM).

INTRODUCTION

A myth echoing through society today contends that real macho men have nothing to do with God. In fact, some people even think of Christian men as sissies. The myth goes on to purport that if a man becomes a believer and lives accordingly, he loses out on life.

Actually, the contrary is true. In this book you'll hear from real men who experience real joy in their lives because of their faith in God. The truth is that the level of pleasure in our lives will be in direct correlation to our faith in God. However, it's also true that those who do follow Jesus choose a road that's often a rough one.

Jesus Christ had to be strong physically in order to live the life He chose. It was no softie who walked by a group of fishermen and said, "Follow me." Without questioning Him, they followed. They were men who made their living pulling heavy fishing nets day and night. It's a profession that requires considerable physical strength. They were real men.

It was a real man who spent 40 days in a rugged desert without food or shelter, as described in Luke 4. Jesus was tender and compassionate, but He was not effeminate in any way. Meekness and weakness are not the same thing. Jesus Christ was every ounce a man, and He found great joy in a life directed by our Heavenly Father. And so can we.

God created us to enjoy His fellowship and the wonderful world He designed for us. When we allow His plan to be fulfilled in our lives, we find ourselves on an incredible journey. We experience joy that those who do not know Him can't imagine. When we follow God's plan, we travel through life on His resources.

Our society has been infected by another myth—that once one

becomes a Christian, the fun in life is over. That's one of Satan's most effective weapons in preventing people from serving Jesus.

The truth, however, is that Jesus came to bring real and lasting *joy* into your life and mine. There is great joy in the forgiveness of our sins. There is joy in knowing that whatever difficulties cross our paths, Jesus will help us get through them.

Heed the apostle Paul's words in Phil. 4:13—"I can do everything through him who gives me strength." Jesus tells us in John 16:33, "In the world you will have tribulation; but be of good cheer, I have overcome the world" (NKJV). Again and again we who serve Jesus experience peace and joy that unbelievers cannot know.

This book is written *by* men *for* men. These are real men from a variety of professions who share situations in their lives that could have been difficult if the joy of the Lord had not been their source of strength. These men have seen firsthand what Jesus meant when He said, "I came so they can have real and eternal life, more and better life than they ever dreamed of" (John 10:10, TM).

Followers of Jesus do not live on the dregs of life. They live in the overflow of His blessings. They have the same problems that all humanity faces. The difference is that as believers they have the help of the same God who parted water, cooled fiery furnaces, closed the mouths of lions to protect His child, and stilled storms on a raging sea to bring peace to His followers. How exciting to know that He has experience in handling any problem we face!

It's significant that more than 275 times the word "rejoice" is used in the Bible. God wants us to have a good time, so He designed life for that purpose. As His children, we have very few limitations placed upon us. We can do anything that's honest, clean, moral, respectful, and kind. We can do anything that does not violate His commandments. That gives us true and lasting freedom.

Enjoy the journey that God has set before you! The writers of these stories testify to the fact that there is *joy* in one's journey with Jesus. They represent many walks of life. You'll meet someone in these pages with whom you can relate as you enjoy the trip of a lifetime. The first step on that journey is to exercise unquestioning faith in God and His Word. Remember, the level of our pleasure in life will be in direct correlation to our faith in God.

—*Gene Williams*

George W. Bush

REMARKS AT THE 2002 NATIONAL PRAYER BREAKFAST

It's a great blessing to have a real man with real faith in Christ as our president of the United States. Working on his ranch in Crawford, Texas, President George W. Bush exemplifies the characteristics our society associates with manhood.

Yet this man's man has a strong faith in God. He has frequently and without apology proclaimed His relationship with our Heavenly Father. In fact, he openly testifies to the changes made in His life because of God's grace. The following statement from his address at the National Prayer Breakfast in 2002 is a clear declaration of the role that real faith has in the life of this real man.

Since we met last year, millions of Americans have been led to prayer. They have prayed for comfort in time of grief, for understanding in a time of anger, for protection in a time of uncertainty. Many, including me, have been on bended knee. The prayers of this nation are a part of the good that has come from the evil of September 11, more good than we could ever have predicted. Tragedy has brought forth the courage and the generosity of our people.

None of us would ever wish on anyone what happened on that day. Yet as with each life, sorrows we would not choose can bring wisdom and strength gained in no other way. This insight is central to many faiths, and certainly to faith that finds hope and comfort in a cross.

Every religion is welcomed in our country; all are practiced here. Many of our good citizens profess no religion at all. Our country has never had an official faith. Yet we have all been witnesses these past 21 weeks to the power of faith to see us through the hurt and loss that has come to our country.

Faith gives the assurance that our lives and our history have a moral design. As individuals, we know that suffering is temporary and hope is eternal. As a nation, we know that the ruthless will not inherit the earth. Faith teaches humility, and with it, tolerance. Once we have recognized God's image in ourselves, we must recognize it in every human being.

Respect for the dignity of others can be found outside of religion, just as intolerance is sometimes found within it. Yet for millions of Americans, the practice of tolerance is a command of faith. When our country was attacked, Americans did not respond with bigotry. People from other countries and cultures have been treated with respect. And this is one victory in the war against terror.

At the same time, faith shows us the reality of good, and the reality of evil. Some acts and choices in this world have eternal consequences. It is always and everywhere wrong to target and kill the innocent. It is always and everywhere wrong to be cruel and hateful, to enslave and oppress. It is always and everywhere right to be kind and just, to protect the lives of others, and to lay down your life for a friend.

The men and women who charged into burning buildings to save others, those who fought the hijackers, were not confused about the difference between right and wrong. They knew the difference. They knew their duty. And we know their sacrifice was not in vain.

Faith shows us the way to self-giving, to love our neighbor as we would want to be loved ourselves. In service to others, we find deep human fulfillment. And as acts of service are multiplied, our nation becomes a more welcoming place for the weak and a better place for those who suffer and grieve.

For half a century now, the National Prayer Breakfast has been a symbol of the vital place of faith in the life of our nation. You've reminded generations of leaders of a purpose and a power greater than their own. In times of calm, and in times of crisis, you've called us to prayer.

In this time of testing for our nation, my family and I have been blessed by the prayers of countless Americans. We have felt their sustaining power, and we're incredibly grateful. Tremendous challenges await this nation, and there will be hardships ahead. Faith will not make our path easy, but it will give us strength for the journey.

The promise of faith is not the absence of suffering; it is the presence of grace. And at every step we are secure in knowing that suffering produces perseverance, and perseverance produces character, and character produces hope—and hope does not disappoint.

May God bless you, and may God continue to bless America.

President Bush's comments can be found in their entirety at <www.whitehouse.gov>.

William H. Frist, M.D.
Majority Leader of the United States Senate
Two Days of Humility

Before becoming a member of the United States Senate, my job was transplanting hearts. A typical night: I was in bed, and the telephone rang. A faceless voice on the other end of the line said, "Dr. Frist, we've got a heart for you. Blood type A. Donor 140 pounds. Sounds like a match for a John Majors."

I received calls like this from the National Organ Donation Registry once or twice a week—usually late at night.

God had answered my first prayer. And the prayers of John Majors.

John was a 55-year-old friend and patient who was dying from severe, rapidly progressive heart disease. In bed and wasting away, a few weeks from certain death, he had waited months for a new heart. He began each day with a prayer that someone, somewhere, would make the gift of a heart so that he could live. With that late-night call, John's prayers were answered. God had blessed him with a second chance at a full life—if my transplant team did a perfect job.

Adrenaline now pumping, I got out of bed, kissed my devoted and understanding wife, Karyn, goodnight, checked on our three sleeping sons, and rushed to the hospital to give John and his wife the good news myself—news I knew they feared they would never hear. Unfortunately, most of my 26 patients who were waiting for a heart would die before a donor heart would become available.

I hurried from home to the hospital to the airport, and an hour later I was on a chartered jet flying through the black night to Chattanooga to remove the healthy heart of a 23-year-old woman who had tragically died hours earlier in a car accident. From the plane, my team jumped into a waiting ambulance, and with lights and sirens blaring, we rushed through the night to a hospital I had never seen to operate alongside surgeons I had never met on a patient I would never have the opportunity to thank.

We scrubbed, opened the chest, and exposed the heart. Every eye in the room focused on that heart—powerful and inspiring as it beat in perfect rhythm, expanding and contracting, pumping blood through thousands of miles of capillaries in the human body. It is a living, vigorous, miracle of God that every second of our lives sustains us with grace and glory.

I cross-clamped the aorta, injected cold cardioplegia into the blood vessels feeding the heart, and instantly the dynamic, magnificently pulsating heart stopped. Suddenly, it was completely motionless—still and quiet. Asleep. That dependable source of energy for physical life, which had not missed a single beat in more than 75 million perfectly timed contractions, was now asleep.

And that's when my own heart began to pound. I began to operate as fast as I could, because starting at that moment we had only four hours to remove the heart, fly back to Nashville, and get it started again in John's body.

A mistake, a delay—anything that took more than four hours, just 240 minutes—meant that this heart would never restart, and John would not see his family in this world again.

Within 10 minutes the heart was removed. I placed it in an Igloo ice chest and dashed to the waiting ambulance. We raced through the night once again, with lights dancing and sirens wailing, to the plane that waited with its engines already expectantly roaring. We roared into Nashville for another bumpy ambulance ride to the hospital, where John was now asleep in the operating room. Carefully, I removed John's old, worn-out, fatally diseased heart and respectfully lowered the young woman's healthy heart into the empty chest cavity.

I sewed the blood vessels together that allowed John's blood to nourish and refill the newly positioned heart.

And then the precious moment of truth arrived—the wait for the heart to come alive again. The room became hushed. Absolute silence. No one moved. No one spoke. This is a precious moment that always, in every case, strikes fear deep in my soul. Will the new heart, suspended now for almost four hours in a lifeless state, come back to life? What if we'd taken too long? What if someone had made a mistake in the blood type? What if I had not done a perfect job in sewing in the new organ? I questioned and doubted everything we did along the way.

This is the dramatic moment when being a heart surgeon is put in perspective. This is when the true meaning of humility rushes to dominate life's playing field. This is when we surgeons realize that we are at best just the riverbed and not the river. This is the moment when God's hand is felt, and His hand is all that matters.

Every time this moment comes, I say a prayer. The prayer is for life. It always includes the 23rd Psalm, "The Lord is my shepherd . . ."

The wait really lasts only a couple of minutes, but, oh, it seems like an eternity. We wait anxiously, with a profound and deep sense of humility, peering down at the flaccid heart, boldly spotlighted by the bright overhead lights, waiting—waiting for that first sign of life. Waiting for rebirth. And more silent prayer. We can do nothing more. It is totally, totally out of our control.

Is there a message to this story? Well, for me it's that whatever we do in life, ultimately, we serve God in whatever way we are so blessed. We don't determine outcome. We don't dictate success. We are just the riverbed for a gloriously flowing and magnificent river.

And what a lesson on giving! The gift is the gift of life from one person to another. A gift is the ultimate expression of love—and the donation of an organ is the ultimate physical gift. Who was that 23-year-old woman whose life was so tragically taken in the auto accident, who acted so selflessly, literally giving of herself so others—whom she had never met and would never know—might live?

All of us try to find ways to give that are within our power. But sometimes we just think about it and don't take action and do it. Although most people don't even like to think about organ donation and try to avoid the subject altogether, organ donation is the ultimate physical gift. The donation of an organ is a gift more powerful than any other—the gift of life. Jesus tells us in John 15 that there is no gift greater than this. He said, "Greater love hath no man than this, that a man lay down his life for his friends" (John 15:13, KJV).

And he also told us to give freely, purely, out of love, without thought of reward: "Be careful not to do your 'acts of righteousness' before men, to be seen by them. . . . When you give . . . do not announce it with trumpets . . . do not let your left hand know what your right hand is doing, so that your giving may be in secret. Then your Father, who sees what is done in secret, will reward you" (Matt. 6:1-4).

There is no gift purer or loftier or more selfless than the gift of a heart or a kidney or a lung. Neither the donor nor his or her family receives or expects anything in return. There are no strings attached. There can't be! And yet the donor, who gives such an intimate and priceless gift, is rewarded with something just as priceless—a gift that transforms a moment of death into new life, transcendent life that continues after physical presence of either donor or recipient.

It's a little like the light of the Lord, which, once shared with another, radiates out from person to person until all within its reach are lit by the fire of love.

This story also says something about miracles. In our everyday lives—climbing out of bed, getting the kids off to school, driving to work, buying groceries, working at the office—miracles often seem like legends left over from childhood. But miracles are not only the stuff of the great stories of the Bible—making the blind see, the lame walk, the dead rise.

Miracles are the manifestation of God in our everyday lives. As a transplant surgeon, I was blessed to see it day after day, week after week, year after year in the operating room. How can an inert piece of muscle, stored in an ice chest for three hours, completely separated from its sustaining blood supply and transported hundreds of miles across the country, explode back to life when placed in another person's body?

Medical scientists can *describe* it, but I can tell you they can't *explain* it. Physicians can *define* it, but they can't *understand* it. Only God knows.

Now, let me shift gears and leap to another day. Imagine flying into the heart of Africa in a single-engine plane, loaded to gross weight with medical supplies, 400 feet above the treetops on the way to a small makeshift hospital in war-torn Sudan.

We're flying low to avoid being sighted by aircraft that indiscriminately and regularly bomb the villages below. We're on a medical mission trip with Dr. Dick Furman, founder of World Medical Mission, and my colleagues from Samaritan's Purse, an international Christian relief organization run by my good friend Franklin Graham.

We land the plane on a dirt strip, drive five bumpy miles along a path past a boarded-up, deserted clinic that has been deserted 12 years prior because of landmines from a prior civil war. We finally arrive at the dilapidated two-room schoolhouse that was converted months earlier into a health clinic.

Prov. 16:9 tells us "In his heart a man plans his course, but the LORD determines his steps."

Indeed, I came to Washington as a public servant in the U.S. Senate, but after arriving, my steps for some inexplicable reason had taken me far from the floor of the Senate on medical mission trips to Africa—to the Congo, Uganda, Kenya, Tanzania, and the Sudan. Six weeks prior to our arrival, Samaritan's Purse courageously opened a small medical clinic in southern Sudan where more than two million people have died and more than four million have been displaced by the war. There is still indiscriminate bombing by aircraft from the north in the region.

We perform surgery where there has been no medical care available for more than a decade. The conditions are very primitive, and there are few surgical instruments. No electricity. No running water. Ether is the only anesthesia. Patients walk or are carried for days when they hear that we are there, for we are the only source of care for hundreds of miles. The civil war has driven off all health care throughout the entire southern Sudan.

The image of that visit I will forever carry with me is of a small, one-room shed next to a schoolhouse that we used as our clinic. The little building was used as a recovery room for the sick and injured. But God's power was at work there.

It was late, and we were just finishing the last operation of a long, tiring day—so long that we completed our last operations under hand-held flashlights. We were scheduled to leave the next day, and I wearily looked forward to returning home. A message came that a patient—a man from the Dinka tribe whom I had never met—wanted to see me, "the American doctor." I just wanted to go to bed, but I went.

Dusk had settled in. I brushed aside the curtain that served as a door. It was pitch-black dark inside. As I approached the voice coming from the corner, I saw the vague silhouette of a man lying in bed. I could see little except the bulky white dressings covering the obvious stump of his left leg and injured right hand. And then I saw his huge smile. It was a smile that pierced the darkness of the room.

Pulling my eyes from that luminous face, I noticed the Bible beside his bed and then the interpreter sitting at his bedside. I asked the patient why he wanted to see "the American doctor." He explained to me that two years ago his wife and two children had been murdered in the civil war. I nodded sympathetically. But that captivating smile seemed to grow even bigger. It was a smile of caring—a smile of love.

His smile seemed to fill the room. How could he smile after losing those he loved most?

Eight days ago, he said, "I lost my leg and fingers when a land mine exploded."

I nodded, still wondering how he smiled. First he lost his family, and now his leg and most of his hand. But his smile grew even broader as we talked about his tragedies. It was a beautiful, shining light in the night.

Finally, I asked, "Why are you smiling—how can you be smiling?"

For two reasons, he explained. "First, because you, Doctor, come to us to share in the spirit of Jesus of Nazareth. And, second, because you are a doctor from America."

I understood the first reason. But I was taken aback by the second. In the transplant medical world I'm accustomed to people thanking me for treating their heart disease—but not because I'm an American.

I asked, "What do you mean, an 'American' doctor?"

Lifting his mutilated limbs for me to see, limbs lost fighting for his own religious freedom, he replied, "Everything I've lost —my family, my leg, my hand—will well be worth the sacrifice if my own people can someday have what you are so blessed to have in America—freedom. The freedom to be and to worship as we please."

That moment was an epiphany of understanding for me. At that moment, in the heart of Africa and in the dark of night and with the words of a man I had never met, I was filled with the enriched perspective that the freedoms and liberties the United States enjoy were obviously not bestowed by people, but have been endowed by our Creator. Our freedom is not based on anything given to us by government but on those inalienable rights bestowed on us by God.

I've been back to the Sudan on a number of medical mission trips. I've operated at the same clinic, now much expanded—though still with no running water—and more developed. I never saw that Dinka man again. But I'll always carry his smile with me.

That smile and his words echoed through my consciousness as I sat on the West Front of the Capitol at the swearing-in of President George W. Bush in January 2001. He reminded us of what a gift we have in freedom, and why it is a gift we must share: "Once a rock in a raging sea, it is now a seed upon the wind, taking root in many nations. It is an ideal we carry but do not own, a trust we bear and pass along."

How true! Man's freedom did not begin with America, but we have an obligation to pass it on. And, as President Bush also reminded us that same day, "*His* purpose is achieved in our duty, and our duty is fulfilled in service to one another."

But what about John Majors?

As we waited breathlessly in the operating room, I prayed that the new heart would be infused with life. The room was silent. No one moved, and all eyes were focused on the motionless, lifeless heart in John's chest.

Suddenly the still heart began to quiver ever so little. Then the quivering began to coarsen into a stronger and stronger ripple. It was coming. Then . . . oomph! The heart suddenly jumped and took a strong and powerful squeezing thrust. In that fraction of a second, the bold, comforting rhythm of life was reborn. Another miracle. Another blessing. And it had all started with a gift.

Orel Hershiser

STARTING TO BELIEVE

When I look back on my minor league baseball career, a jumble of impressions hits me. I was one of about ten new draftees added to the Clinton, Iowa, Class A club. Fresh meat. We were coming, and other guys were going, their dreams dashed. I'll never forget taking the locker of a guy who had just left with his belongings in his bag, his eyes vacant. "Hey!" someone hollered at him. "The new guy's gonna need your hat and stirrups!" Without a word, he fished them out and tossed them to me. I wondered if I would be doing the same thing some day, heading home with a memory, a story for the grandkids about a chance I once had with the Dodgers.

More important than anything else in my minor league career were two friends I met. One I have since lost track of and would like to hook up with again sometime. The other has promised to love me and let me live with Him forever.

Butch Wickensheimer was a teammate at Clinton. He intrigued me. When the rest of us were out having a good time, he was relaxing, reading his Bible, and staying sober—a nice guy. We kidded him about being "religious," but he wasn't obnoxious about it. He didn't let anyone interfere with his own convictions. On the team bus, he would try to sit under a light that was working so he could read his Bible. I asked him what he saw in it.

"Everything," he told me. "It's God's gift to man. It tells how much He loves us and how we can know Him." That sounded all right. I had a Bible. It was in the bottom drawer of my dresser at home, where it had been all my life. I went to church on Easter and Christmas, and they had Bibles in the pews, so I didn't need to take mine. When did I read it? Never. I believed in God and Adam and Eve and heaven. People went to heaven if they were good. Christians were good.

Butch had a different idea. He didn't push me, but when I asked, he would explain what the Bible said about heaven. People who are simply good don't go there—*forgiven* people do. There was nothing I could do to qualify for heaven. I was a sinner, just like everybody else. The only perfect Person who ever lived was Jesus, and He had taken the punishment for sin. The only way to God was through Jesus. You had to receive Him, make Him your Savior.

"Where does it say that?" I asked.

"John 14:6 and Eph. 2:8-9," Butch said. When no one was around, I looked those verses up in a Gideon-placed Bible in my hotel room. It took me half an hour to find them, because I didn't know how the Bible was arranged.

Sure enough, that's what it said. I wanted to argue with Butch about it, but I didn't want the other guys to see me talking to him too much. They might get the wrong idea. They might put me in the Christian athlete category.

I played devil's advocate with Butch. I asked him everything from how he knew there was a God and how he knew the Bible was really from God—to what happens to children if they die before they become Christians. I was looking for an out. I needed a reason to say it wasn't for me. If I could find some major problem with it, some big inconsistency, I could say then that I had made a decision. That decision would be no, and I could quit thinking about it, quit talking about it.

When the season was over and I went back home, I dug my Bible out and read more. *This is what Butch reads every day,* I told myself. *Amazing.*

I had made a decent start in my career, winning four and losing none, and Butch and I had both been selected to attend the Arizona Instructional League in the fall. That was a big deal to me, because only a few players from each minor league team were assigned. I asked if Butch could be one of my roommates at the Buckaroo Hotel in Scottsdale. Out there I quizzed him more and more. How could this be? What about that? Explain this. Answer that. He was patient, and he was consistent. His answers always came from the Bible.

I finally realized that Butch was limited. He could answer questions and point out verses, but he couldn't convince me. He couldn't make the decision for me. I was going to have to accept Christianity or reject it. More specifically, Butch explained, it was Christ I was deciding about. Was He just a man, a good teacher, as so many say? And how could He be called a good teacher if He himself claimed to be God and wasn't? What kind of a teacher is that?

I wasn't a big-time scoundrel, but I knew my life would change if I bought into this. It was no minor matter. Did it make sense to me? Could I accept what I understood and take the rest by faith? Or was there still a way out? Could I point to disasters and catastrophes and somehow blame God and thereby ease my conscience?

Butch said God loved me and wanted a relationship with me. What could that mean? Could I know God? Could God know me? God was perfect, and I wasn't. I was just a guy, and He was, well—God. How could I relate to Him? Butch said Jesus was the answer. I could relate to Him, because even though He was perfect, He had also become a man. He was the bridge. He had paid for my sin. If I could accept that and believe in Christ, then I could be forgiven and know I was a child of God and going to heaven.

It took a long time to sink in. Sometimes, just when I was

thinking it sounded pretty good, I would catch myself. *You're not really thinking about this, are you?* I would ask myself. *Are you starting to believe it?* I would be one of the guys for a while, and then I would gravitate back toward Butch, asking more and more questions.

I almost wore out the poor guy with all my skepticism and badgering. Down deep I knew it was my decision. There was no more to ask. I was tired of making up questions he couldn't answer just so I could prove him wrong and not have to believe. I had to do something about the sin problem that he showed me in Rom. 3:23. Since there was nothing I could personally do about it, I had to make a decision about John 3:16. If all have sinned, I'm included. And if those who believe in Jesus can live forever, well, the only thing left to decide was whether or not I believed that.

One September night at the Buckaroo, I was the only one in the room. I had pulled out the Bible there in my room and was reading the Book of John. My mind was racing. Do I believe in God? Yes. Do I believe the Bible is God's message to humanity? Yes. Do I believe what the Bible says? Yes. That all have sinned? Yes. That nothing I can do can save me from my sin? Yes. That Jesus already did it for me and that He is the only way to God? Yes. Do I want Christ in my life? Do I want to become a Christian?

I slipped off the bed and knelt beside it. How does one go about praying? I didn't know. I figured if God was God, He would understand if I just told Him what was on my mind. I said, *God, I don't know everything about You. I don't think I ever will. But I know I'm a sinner, and I know I want to be forgiven. I know I want Christ in my life, and I want to go to heaven. I want to become a Christian. With that, I accept You. Amen.*

No tears, no lightning, no wind, no visions. I just got back onto the bed and continued reading the Bible. What a relief! I knew I had done the right thing. I had stepped from skepticism to belief. God had forgiven me, and Christ was in me, and the character He had already built into me affected the type of a Christian I would become. I was an all-or-nothing kind of a guy. This wasn't something I had simply taken care of and gotten out of the way. I was into this all the way. I wanted to quit pretending to be happy about other players' success when secretly I wanted to be the only one doing well. I wanted to quit living a lie and be genuinely thrilled when a teammate was called up to the big leagues.

Almost immediately God gave me a genuine love and compassion for people. I could be happy for someone else without suffering myself. God impressed upon me that He would take care of me and love me no matter what. Whether I made the big leagues and became rich and famous and had everything the world has to offer or I failed at baseball, He would be there.

When Butch got in, I told him, "I accepted the Lord tonight, and I really feel good about it." He was as matter-of-fact as I was. I know he was thrilled for me, but in his own way he simply let me know what the next steps were. He recommended a lot of Bible reading, especially in passages that were meaningful to him when he was a new Christian. He said I should get into a Bible study, start going to a church that believed and taught the Bible, spend time with other Christians, and start telling other people about my decision.

My faith was very personal. It meant everything to me. I checked against the Bible every new thing I heard. I let the Bible speak to me. When I went home at the end of the instructional league, I was impressed with how much Christmas meant to me for the first time in my life.

Adapted from *Between the Lines: Nine Principles to Live By,* by Orel Hershiser. Copyright © 2001 by Orel Leonard Hershiser IV. Used by permission of Warner Books, Inc.

Orel Hershiser went on from that experience to become one of the greatest pitchers in major league baseball. He not only climbed from minor league ball to the top of the major leagues—he also became a major-league Christian. The year 1988, when he was named most valuable player of the National League Play-offs and the World Series and won the Cy Young Award, was a great and memorable time in his life. But the miracle of grace in his spiritual life continues to give him the greatest joy.

Orel Hershiser *pitched for the Los Angeles Dodgers, where he was a National League Cy Young Award winner. He was also named Most Valuable Player for the National League Championship Series and the 1988 World Series.* Sports Illustrated *chose him as Sportsman of the Year, and the Associated Press named him Professional Athlete of the Year. He and his wife, Jamie, have three sons.*

Philip Fulmer

STILL A WORK IN PROGRESS

I lived a typical small-town existence as a boy growing up. I had loving parents who saw to it that I received proper guidance. Even though we had little money, we had lots of love, a strong work ethic, and a deep appreciation for family. Church was a major focus of our tightly knit family. My aunts, uncles, and grandparents, along with my mom and dad, saw to it that my emotional and spiritual needs were met.

Adversities and challenges confronted us along the way, but we had it really good when it came to my strong family. My greatest memory is of all the love I felt—and still feel—from my mother and father. But even greater security and love were always present from my Heavenly Father.

When I went to college, I was like many other students. I didn't always make the best choices or the wisest decisions. I struggled sometimes with setting priorities and finding the right balance in my life. Although my faith remained strong, my day-to-day habits drifted toward what was popular and the most fun, and sometimes those things were not in harmony with my Christian roots.

But God is good, and He's always there when we call on Him. He led me to teammates in college, as He had in high school, who were there to keep me accountable and on the right track. Steve Robinson and John Keller wouldn't let me get far from the path that Christ walked with me. As my parents had done for my first 17 years, my peers, armed with immense faith, directed me back toward the light. I thank God for these men.

My first job after college was at Wichita State University, and it was quite a challenge. In 1970 half of the Wichita State football team died in an airplane crash in Colorado. Our assignment was to resurrect the program, and it was not easy to coach in that situation. But as He had done during every challenge of my life, God put a special person in my life to guide me spiritually. John Stucky was my office mate, my roommate for a while, my constant companion, and a strong, quiet, spiritual advisor.

John continues to be a strong man of God today. He taught me the importance of a quiet time every day, how to study the Word of God through passages in the Bible, and how to share my faith with others. I have vivid memories of the hours we spent talking about life and our place in it.

In 1993 when I became head coach at the University of Tennessee, I asked John to join the staff as the strength and conditioning coach. That was one of the best decisions I ever made. Although he has had some health issues to deal with lately, for nine years he was the spiritual strength of Tennessee football. He was a strong contributor to the Tennessee football team's most winning era. John touched lives everywhere he went, and he had a strong impact on the Volunteer football team.

In January 1999 I had the thrill of coaching Tennessee to victory over Florida State in the Fiesta Bowl at Tempe, Arizona, and we were declared national champions. I won't say that God loved us more than He loved the Seminoles, but He surely was with us that day.

As thrilling as that win was, though, it wasn't the greatest joy I've ever experienced. My greatest joy continues to come from the privilege of working with the young men God has placed in my care.

Every day I thank God for the blessings He has bestowed on me—and there are many. I'm grateful for my parents and grandparents and the love of my family. I'm thankful for the men in my community of Winchester, Tennessee, who went out of their way to minister to me when I was young. I'm thankful to coaches who shared the Word of God with me and prayed with me and my teammates after games. I'm grateful for friends who have kept me on track throughout my life. And I'm so grateful for a devoted Christian wife who loves me. Being the wife of the head football coach at a major university is a challenge, and she has been more than equal to the challenge.

I'm still coaching at the University of Tennessee, and I'm privileged to share in a Bible study that continues to feed my mind and spirit with God's Word. I work and fulfill my role as a husband, father, and coach. But my greatest desire is to be a true and obedient servant to God.

I'm still a work in progress. God has been so faithful to me and has given me such joy that I can hardly wait to see where He takes me next.

Philip Fulmer *is head football coach at the University of Tennessee. His 1998 team won the Southeast Conference championship. As a coach, he holds one of the five best win/loss records in college football history. He has been chosen as national and Southeast Conference coach of the year. Philip and his wife, Vicky, live in Knoxville, Tennessee. They have four children.*

Bill Gaither
MORE THAN THE MUSIC

Growing up in the quiet rural community of Alexandria, Indiana, Bill Gaither had an insatiable appetite for gospel music. His consuming interest in high school was to attend the Stamps Quartet School of Music—the largest such school in America—that was held each June in Dallas, Texas. While Bill was not gifted with an outstanding singing voice, his brother, Danny, was. It was the combination of consuming love for gospel music and opportunity to go to the Stamps School along with a gifted brother that launched an outstanding career. Bill writes about that in his book It's More than the Music.

I could hardly wait to finish my final year of high school, and I worked every spare hour to save enough money to return to the Stamps School of Music the following summer after graduation in 1954. Once again, I sang with Charlie Hodge at the Stamps school, and with all the enthusiasm three weeks of solid gospel singing can evoke, Charlie and I came back home convinced we could develop a career in gospel music. Charlie had a friend from Alabama who sang bass, so they, Danny, and I formed a gospel singing group known as the Pathfinders.

We sang at churches, fairs, and just about anywhere anyone would invite us in Indiana. Sometimes we got paid, sometimes we didn't. Often when we sang in churches, the congregation would take up a freewill love offering on our behalf. I learned quickly that it's hard to live on love.

We heard that Illinois held some good opportunities for a group like ours, so we made the big jump across the state line.

When we found that things were no better there, we later moved to Columbus, Ohio. When we made the first move, Danny had to drop out of the group because he had two years of high school remaining. We replaced him with another fellow who was a good singer but not nearly as good as Danny. I knew I'd miss singing with my brother, but it was time to get out of the cornfields and into the big time. I was 19 years of age and ready to conquer the world.

In an effort to duplicate the success of the Dixie Four, we talked our way onto a 15-minute radio show that Pennington Bread Sponsored on WRFD in Worthington, Ohio. We hoped that people would hear us on the show, invite us to sing at their churches or civic functions, and throngs of excited gospel music lovers would turn out.

They didn't.

In fact, they avoided the Pathfinders in droves. Looking back, I can see that the Pathfinders were four young guys with a lot of enthusiasm, a little potential, and even less raw talent. When I compare our sound to that of The Statesmen or The Blackwood Brothers, we left a lot to be desired. But at the time, we thought we were hot stuff and even shared the stage with some big-name quartets as the opening acts when they came to town.

For more than eight months, the Pathfinders struggled along, hoping and believing that around the next turn we were going to make it, yet not knowing where our next meal was going to come from. On more than a few occasions, I recall surviving on nothing more than toast and coffee. We worked hard, we promoted ourselves aggressively, but the success we sought continued to elude us. For some reason, the group just wasn't working. We weren't good enough for any concert promoters—what few there were in those days—to get excited about us as musicians; we weren't entertaining showmen; we didn't have a deep powerful spiritual impact. We were just four young guys who loved to sing. We didn't have that intangible quality that athletes refer to as "chemistry' or show people call "magic." We were missing whatever it took to make us more than music.

One August afternoon at a country fairgrounds in the small town of Van Wert, Ohio, the Pathfinders were at a dead end. Broke, dejected, and discouraged, we were scheduled to perform a concert at the 4-H building that night. When we heard how many tickets had been sold for our concert, the number was so negligible that had I not been so close to tears, I probably would have laughed uproariously.

But the joke was on us. I felt nauseated and disheartened. As I trudged out behind the 4-H building to get some air and sort through my thoughts, my heart was breaking. All my lofty dreams, my inflated hopes and plans to be a career gospel singer seemed to be nothing more than hot air. Reality was pinching at my idealism, and the balloon was about to pop. Salty tears flowed freely down my face, and I didn't even bother wiping them away. I had never felt so low in all my life. I was an abject failure, with no money, no career, no future.

Reluctantly yet resolutely, I hung up my dream of being a professional gospel musician. I've always been a realist, and for the first time in my life I had to confront the ugly truth that I was not good enough—not good enough to be a professional singer, not good enough to be a professional piano player, not smart enough or manipulative enough to make it in the real world of professional music.

All I could do was pray.

Nowadays, I'm aware that prayer can be more than my last resort, but back then I wasn't tuned in to God very well. I had grown up going to our home church in Alexandria, Indiana, and I believed in God. I'd asked the Lord to come into my life nearly every summer at church camp, as well as several times when traveling preachers had come by our town to conduct revivals. I tried to live in a manner pleasing to God as best as I knew how. But my spirituality was based mostly on emotional experiences rather than a commitment to and genuine relationship with God. Undoubtedly, for a while after each revival or similar spiritual event I attended, I felt energized. I tried to live a little better. But I was still the one in control. I called the shots; I did what I wanted to do and made my own decisions. Even my dreams of being a gospel musician were more about me than they were about God or the gospel. I just wanted to make a living doing something I enjoyed.

But behind that 4-H building that day, I came to the end of myself, my way, my ability or lack of it, my trying to make something happen. And for the first time, I truly placed my life into God's hands.

I prayed, *God, there has to be more to life than this. I don't know what You want me to do, but evidently, it's not music. So I don't know how I'm going to make a living, but I'm not going to do this anymore.* I committed myself to doing whatever God had planned, even though at that point I had no clue what that might be. *God, if music is not what You want for me, I'm willing to give it up,* I said. I winced at the words. Even as I prayed, I was convinced that my music career was over.

I was confused and perplexed, but I wasn't angry with God. After all, I hadn't really consulted with Him about entering the music field; I'd just followed my dream the way everyone says a person is supposed to do. Now that my reality check had decimated me, I laid down my dreams, never imagining that my utter failure could be the beginning of the fulfillment of His dreams for me.

Where do you go when your dreams have been dashed, when your hopes are all gone? Where do you go when you have nowhere else to go?

You run to those who love you unconditionally.

At the lowest point of my 19 years, I decided to go home. The morning after the Van Wert concert disaster, I told the rest of the guys in the group, "I'm going home."

At first the guys tried to talk me into staying a little longer. "Things are just starting to gel, Bill," one of the guys said. "Don't give up now."

"We're almost there, Bill," another guy said. "A few more concerts and we'll be over the hump."

I had been hearing such things for months now, but the truth was that there was not a large-enough audience who wanted to hear what we were doing. It didn't make me a bad person or the guys a poor group. It was simply a matter of timing and talent.

I got in my car and drove back to Alexandria, where Mom and Dad welcomed me. They didn't criticize, condemn, or chastise me. My folks were so supportive! They didn't say, "Bill, we told you that music thing wasn't going to work." Nor did they say anything like "Well, it's about time you came to you senses!" I can never remember any attitude from my parents other than loving support, open arms, and acceptance.

That's not to say that other people within our circle of friends and family members didn't regard my dream-chasing as foolish. Although he never mentioned it to me at the time, Dad took quite a razzing from people who wondered why I wasn't out looking for a real job. Frequently friends of relatives who didn't quite understand my passion to perform gospel music asked Dad, "How's Bill doing?" They *knew* how Bill was doing. He was falling on his face! But Dad was always kind and gracious.

Dad was cool. "Well, he's struggling," he replied. "And he's struggling pretty hard. I don't think they're going to make it."

"What's he going to do?" the relatives asked.

"I don't know," Dad answered pensively. "We'll just have to wait and see."

But when I stepped through the doors of our little home,

Mom and Dad were right there for me, eager to help me pick up the pieces and start over again. Mom and Dad never really stated it, but all the Gaither kids knew: no matter where we'd been or what we'd done—good or bad—we could always come home.

I returned to my hometown and to my job at Cox's, the local grocery store, waiting on shoppers and working as a meat-cutter in the butcher shop. It didn't take me long to figure out that I was not born to be a meat-cutter, so I did one of the smartest things I've ever done in my life. I decided to enroll in college. I applied to and was accepted at Taylor University, a Christian liberal arts school in Upland, Indiana, but I kept my job at Cox's to help pay my tuition.

I knew nothing about college; I knew little of the joy of learning, grappling with new or controversial ideas, or approaching life from a philosophical worldview. Nobody else in the Gaither family had ever gone to college. My only interests outside of music were in English literature: in high school, I had been an average student in most other courses, but in music and English, I excelled. So when it came time to choose a college major, I wrote down "English lit."

I continued living at home in Alexandria and commuted every day to Taylor. It was a half-hour drive, so to pass the time each morning I tuned my car radio to WOWO, the 50,000-watt blowtorch broadcasting a show featuring the Weatherford Quartet from Fort Wayne, Indiana. That was about the only gospel music I heard during my tenure at Taylor, since Southern gospel was not considered an acceptable style of church music at that time. But even if it wasn't in the churches or in the school's curriculum, the music was in my blood. I listened to gospel music like a castaway craving water.

While I enjoyed studying English and literature, I found the rest of my academic studies somewhat boring. Nevertheless, I worked hard and tried to make the most of my college experience.

I was just getting comfortable with the whole idea of college when one day, out of the blue, Earl Weatherford and his wife, Lily, stopped by Alexandria and offered me a job playing piano for their group. They had heard me play at the Stamps School of Music and then later with the Pathfinders, and they were convinced I could contribute to the Weatherfords.

I could hardly believe my ears as I listened to their offer. The Weatherford Quartet wanted me! Better still, they were willing to pay me more money to play piano for them than I made cutting meat at the grocery store. I told the Weatherfords that I'd talk it over with my parents and call them as soon as possible.

When I broached the idea of leaving college to travel with the Weatherfords, Dad was clearly troubled. An easygoing father who rarely declined any reasonable request from his children, Dad surprised me. "No, Bill," he said. "You've started at Taylor, and you're going to finish."

That was some of the best advice I've ever received in my life. I tell aspiring artists something similar today: "Finish your education first. Even though the lure of diesel smoke is strong and enticing, the tour bus will still be there after you get your education."

I tell parents of talented offspring the same thing.

Truth is, I am able to operate at the level I do within the music community not because of luck or unusual musical ability but largely because I stayed in school and finished my formal education. Many talented artists discover too late that it takes more than an attractive appearance, hot vocal licks, or cute little ditties to last in the music business, especially once you pass certain age milestones.

I respected my dad immensely, and I knew better than to argue with him. As much as he had always supported me in pursuing my dreams of being a gospel musician, we had already been down that road, and it had gone nowhere. He had seen how difficult and unstable making a living could be in that line of work. Not surprisingly, he wanted me to complete my college education before heading out on any more wild goose chases—even if it meant turning down the offer of going with the Weatherfords.

I reluctantly called the Weatherfords and declined their kind offer. When I got off the phone, a sick feeling ran through my stomach. *I've just closed the door on an offer of a lifetime,* I thought. Most of my friends from the Stamps School of Music would have been thrilled to be on stage with the Weatherfords, and what had I done? I'd turned them down to study English literature and poetry!

It's often said that for a Christian the tough decisions are not so much between good and bad but between *good* and *best*. I didn't know it then, of course, but to have gone with the Weatherfords would have been a great honor, lots of fun, and probably an exhilarating experience for me—but it would not have been God's best for my life. As much as I will always be grateful for Earl and Lily's confidence in me when I had so little confidence in myself, I'm thankful to Dad and to the Lord for keeping me in school. God had a much bigger plan in mind than *I* had!

From *It's More than Music: Life Lessons for Loving God, Loving Each Other* by Bill Gaither. Copyright © 2003 by The Gaither Charitable Foundation, Inc. By permission of Warner Books, Inc.

Bill Gaither *is considered by many as the most successful and honored artist in the history of Christian music. For more than 30 years as a composer, songwriter and producer, Bill has received 4 Grammys, 20 Dove Awards, and the first Gold Record ever awarded to an inspirational album. He was inducted into the Gospel Music Association Hall of Fame in 1983. Bill was recently honored by ASCAP as Christian Songwriter of the Century. He still lives in Alexandria, Indiana, with his wife, Gloria.*

Franklin Graham

THE REBEL

In July 1974 the Billy Graham Evangelistic Association sponsored the International Congress for Evangelism in Lausanne, Switzerland. About 2,500 Protestant Evangelical leaders came from 150 countries to attend the 10-day conference.

I left for Switzerland in May, right after I graduated from Montreat-Anderson College, to help handle logistics for the congress.

I had spent the summer in that area when I was young, so it was familiar territory. I rented a small apartment for the summer. Actually, to call it "small" is being generous. It was more like a room, eight feet wide and fifteen feet long. The bathtub was so tiny that I had to sit on a ledge in the tub and use a long shower hose to rinse off.

Trying to cook was another hardship and a brand-new experience for me. I had watched Bea [a family friend who lived in the Graham home] fry chicken enough that I didn't think there would be anything to it. So I went to the market and bought a whole chicken, which I had to cut up into pieces myself. I threw some flour, salt, and pepper into a paper bag along with the chicken parts, just as Bea had done so many times. I shook hard, but I didn't remember Bea getting the flour all over the place the way I managed to do.

But that wasn't nearly as big a mess as when I filled the frying pan with oil and turned the heat on high. I dumped the chicken into the hot grease, and it spattered, popped, and smoked. (I usually liked things that popped and smoked, but not this time!) I was very discouraged five minutes later when I took the charred chicken out of the sizzling grease. I couldn't figure out why it was overdone on the outside and raw on the inside. So much for bachelor life!

When I returned to my apartment from my work each evening, I had no television set or stereo equipment to turn on, so I started reading my New Testament. Even though I was living one adventure after another, I felt such emptiness. I had friends, but still I was lonely and unfulfilled. Something just didn't connect in my life. It was like having a television set but not plugging it in.

The sinful life I was living was not satisfying me any longer. There was this emptiness, a big hole right in the middle of Franklin Graham's life, a void that needed to be filled. The truth is, I felt miserable, because my life wasn't right with God.

During the Lausanne conference I celebrated my 22nd birthday. Mama and Daddy wanted to take me to lunch. "Where do you want to go?" Daddy asked.

I chose a little Italian restaurant on Lake Geneva. Nothing much happened during the meal. It was pleasant and relaxed. We had a good time.

After that meal, Daddy and I walked along a pathway beside the lake. My father, who hates confrontation, turned to me and somewhat nervously said, "Franklin, your mother and I sense there's a struggle going on in your life."

I stared at him but didn't say anything. He had caught me totally off guard. *How does he know this?* I wondered.

"You're going to have to make a choice either to accept Christ or reject Him," he continued. "You can't continue to play the middle ground. Either you're going to choose to follow and obey Him, or you'll reject Him."

My mind raced. *What's he going to say next?*

"I want you to know we're proud of you, Franklin. We love you no matter what you do in life and no matter where you go.

The door of our home is always open, and you're always welcome. But you're going to have to make a choice."

I felt angry. Maybe I was mad because he had seen right through me. I had always thought I was so clever and could fool my parents. After all, I went to church, sang the hymns, and said the right words. But my sinful life was no secret. I couldn't figure out how he knew about the struggle that had been going on inside me for some time. But he did—and I knew he was right.

After he had his say, Daddy patted my shoulder and smiled. He said nothing more about it as we finished our walk.

But in spite of some of the most beautiful and inspiring scenery in the world—and near the man I loved and wanted to please more than anyone else on earth—I felt joyless, empty, lonely, and dirty. The clock was ticking loudly now on my own personal "hour of decision."

The congress ended a few days later. I bolted from Switzerland to help Roy Gustafson conduct the last summer tour. Daddy had paid for David Hill to come to the congress and wanted him to travel with me on Roy's tour to the Middle East. I think Daddy thought David was a young Christian who would benefit from Roy's Bible teaching, so David and I flew to Zurich to meet Roy.

The first stop on the tour was Rome. One evening, while we were at the Cavaleri Hilton, I went to David's room and found him reading his Bible.

"Hey, kid," he said. "What's going on?"

I said, "Not much. What are you doing?"

"Just reading what the apostle Paul has to say in Romans 7— want to hear it?" David asked.

"Guess so," I replied, figuring I didn't have much choice.

David read, "I have *the will* to do good, but not *the power*. That is, I don't accomplish the good I set out to do, and the evil I don't really want to do I find I am always doing" (Rom. 7:18-19, PHILLIPS, emphasis added). David paused.

I felt like that deep down inside. I couldn't believe that the apostle Paul had had the same struggles.

"No Christian is perfect," David said. "None of us has the power or the ability to live a life of absolute perfection—not even Paul. But when we let Jesus Christ come into our hearts and we surrender our lives to Him, He gives us the power to live the Christian life because of His Spirit living in us."

David had my attention. He went on: "I *want* to do good, [but in *practice* I do] evil. . . . [This is in] continual conflict with [my conscious attitude and makes me an unwilling prisoner]" (Rom. 7:21, 23, PHILLIPS, emphasis added).

This was me! I wanted to do right. I wanted to get my life cleaned up—but how? Daddy had told me a few days earlier that I had to make a choice. But how could I? The apostle Paul confessed his weakness. Could *I*?

David continued: "It is an [agonizing] situation, and who can set me free from the prison of my mortal body? I thank God there is a way out through Jesus Christ our Lord" (Rom. 7:24-25, PHILLIPS).

I felt frustrated as I listened, wondering how to overcome such a struggle. I broke out in a sweat and lit a cigarette to ease the tension.

David didn't say another word at that moment—he just stared at me. I think he knew that God was speaking to me. I made some excuse to leave, but I couldn't forget the words David had just read.

How many times had I heard these verses? But this time they sounded as if the apostle Paul had written them in a personal letter to me. I realized for the first time that sin had control over my life. Franklin Graham was not in charge—sin was. And there was absolutely nothing I could do in my own power to overcome it. I went back to my room, fished through my luggage for my New Testament, and turned to Rom. 8:1—"There is therefore now no condemnation to those who are in Christ Jesus."

No condemnation for those in Christ, I thought. I was condemned; I had broken God's law in every conceivable way, and it troubled me. I wanted what David Hill had. I wanted what Roy Gustafson had. I wanted what my parents had.

That night instead of going to the bar for a couple of beers, I found myself alone in my room reading through the Gospel of John.

When I came to the third chapter, I read not just that Jesus told Nicodemus he had to be born again, but I also grasped that Franklin Graham had to be born again as well. (See John 3:3-7.)

I don't remember all that happened that night, but when I went to bed, I knew that not all was well with Franklin Graham. Something was missing in my life. I was the son of Billy Graham, I went to church, and I memorized Scripture. What more did it take to be a Christian? My mind raced, and I found myself talking as though there were two people struggling inside of me. I don't remember getting much sleep.

For the next several days I didn't have much time to myself because of the demands of the tour. We had gone on to Israel, and on our fourth night in the country, we stayed at a hotel in Jerusalem.

I went to my room early. I sat on my bed and smoked a cigarette, picked up my New Testament, and reread John 3. The words of my father a few weeks earlier haunted me: "Franklin, you're going to have to make a choice either to accept Christ or to reject Him." I thought back to the time I had made a decision for Christ at age eight. I'm not sure I really understood what I had done. All I knew was that Franklin Graham was a sinner who had been running from God. Suddenly I had an overpowering conviction that I needed to get my life right with God.

I read John 3 again, in which Jesus told Nicodemus, "You must be born again." Nicodemus was a respected religious leader in his city. Yet all his religion and learning were not enough to gain entrance into heaven. Nicodemus had to be *born again.* All I knew was that I wanted the big empty hole inside of me to be filled. I was tired of running.

I read Rom. 8:1 over and over, and I realized that I was not "in" Christ. More than anything else, I wanted to be—but I didn't know how.

I put my cigarette out and got down on my knees beside my bed. I'm not sure what I prayed, but I know that I poured my heart out to God and confessed my sin. I told Him I was sorry and that if He would take the pieces of my life and somehow put them back together, I was His. I wanted to live my life for Him from that day forward. I asked Him to forgive me and cleanse me, and I invited Him by faith to come into my life.

That night I finally decided that I was sick and tired of being sick and tired. My years of running and rebellion had ended.

I got off my knees and went to bed.

It was finished.

The rebel had found the cause.

Adapted from Franklin Graham, *Rebel with a Cause* (Nashville: Thomas Nelson Publishers, 1995). Used by permission.

Franklin Graham *is president and chief executive officer of Samaritan's Purse and the Billy Graham Evangelistic Association. He is the author of numerous books and travels the world as an evangelist. He and his wife, Jane Austin, have four children. They live in Boone, North Carolina.*

Reggie White
How to Have a Miracle

I have seen miracle after miracle in the trenches—not just the miracle of being able to play with an injured elbow, knee, or hamstring. I have seen far greater miracles than these. The greatest miracle of all is that of a changed life, the miracle of guys who used to curse with every other word, who used to abuse alcohol and drugs, who used to treat women as if they were only toys for their own pleasure—suddenly having their lives completely transformed and cleansed. I believe a miracle always begins with prayer. I learned this fact at an early age, even before I became a Christian. Not surprisingly, I learned this lesson while I was involved in competitive sports.

I was 10 years old. Though I had played football in the Dixie Youth League, I was afraid of being hurt, of being hit too hard by the older guys who were bigger and tougher than I was. So I joined a baseball league, figuring I was a lot less likely to get tackled and hurt on a baseball diamond than on a football field. One time we played against a team with a really good pitcher. I mean, that kid had a fastball that wouldn't quit, and I could never get a hit off him. I came up to bat late in the game with two, maybe three, guys on base. I remember the pitcher intentionally walking the batter ahead of me, saying that I was going to be an "easy out."

Understand that I didn't believe God answers the prayers of children. No one had ever taught me that God answers only grown-up prayers; it was just a mind-set I had. Even so, I figured there was no way I was going to hit the next pitch without some sort of outside help—so I prayed: *God, if You answer the prayers of children, help me hit a home run—please.* I stepped into the batter's box and raised my bat. The first two balls hummed right over the plate—strike one, strike two. *Well, I guess God answers only the prayers of grown-ups,* I thought.

The pitcher zipped the third pitch, and I connected. I opened my eyes, and—man, that ball was gone! I mean, I hit it far. I was so shocked that I sprinted around the bases, because I didn't know if it was a home run or not. Then I heard the coach holler, "Slow down, White! You hit a home run!" Some of the guys who went to get the ball came back and told me, dead serious, that the ball had dug a hole into the ground where it hit. I knew that a 10-year-old kid couldn't hit a ball like that by himself. That's when I knew that it must have been God. Three years later, at age 13, I turned my life over to Jesus Christ.

Now why would God give 10-year-old Reggie White a home run? Did He like me more than the kid who threw the pitch? No way. God doesn't play favorites. Neither is He a genie in the bottle who exists to do our bidding and perform miracles at our command. God is God, and He will demonstrate or withhold His power according to His plan and His timetable, not ours. He doesn't exist to do our will; we exist to do His.

But there is a very simple, obvious principle involved in the realm of miracles: You don't get if you don't ask. Admittedly, some miracles have happened to me that I hadn't asked for—but somebody had. When God healed my sprained elbow, it wasn't because of my prayers, because I didn't think God was going to heal me. Other people prayed, and God responded to their prayers in a mighty way.

God doesn't always answer prayer in the way we want or expect. He doesn't always answer according to our schedule. Sometimes we think His watch is slow, when ours is actually running way fast. There have been times I've prayed for selfish things, and God has said no to those prayers—and ultimately I was always glad that He did. There have been times I've prayed and gotten quite frustrated, thinking, *Man, I must be doing something wrong, because God isn't paying any attention to me.* I later found out that He was listening, He was active, He was answering my prayer—but first He wanted to teach me something through the waiting period. Sometimes prayer is just a matter of persistence; God wants to know that we're dedicated to seeking Him over the long haul.

I think sometimes we misunderstand prayer. We treat it as a ritual or a chore. Or we think it's only about our talking to God—*Lord, You need to listen to what I say, now!*—and we forget to *listen* to God. Some of my best times alone with God in prayer have been those spent not on my knees but in an easy chair or flat on my back, with no agenda, no list of "gimmes" or "I-wants." Sometimes I fall asleep just basking in the presence of God, absorbing His love, saying nothing, asking for nothing. I believe God wants us to relax in His presence and enjoy fellowship with Him. He sometimes wants us to simply sit down, shut up, and listen—not just with our minds but with our feelings.

Oh, there are times when we need to get on our knees before God—but the Bible talks about men and women of faith who simply prostrated themselves before Him. Why shouldn't we do the same? Why shouldn't we sit down, lie down in the grass, take a walk by the lake in the presence of God? When we talk to God, listen to Him, and meditate on Him, why shouldn't we relax? What's to stop us from praying in our cars or at a football game or while we're hugging our children?

Indeed, prayer should be two-way communication. There have been times when God has spoken to me when I was simply watching television. I've been disturbed by what I've seen on the screen and realized that this was God's Spirit in me reacting to these events, speaking to me, revealing His will to me.

For example, when I say that God spoke to me about how to heal the division between the races, I'm not saying He spoke to me at a single moment in time; rather, He spoke to me over a period of months or years, often through newspapers and television news broadcasts, making clear to me His perspective on the events that are going on around us and focusing those events through the lens of His Word, the Bible.

God has given me a ministry of healing. Recently I've assisted in healing services where we've seen people healed of back problems, cataracts, cancer, drug addiction, and emotional affliction. I personally know of one man we prayed for who was scheduled for cancer surgery and even with the surgery was given only six months to live. The doctors put him onto the table, opened him up, and found the cancer had dried up to a little spit. The doctors couldn't believe it. They said, "This guy's going to live," and he's alive and healthy today.

One lady we prayed for had cataracts. When we prayed for her eyes, she believed God had healed her. She wanted to get proof to show others, so a few days later she went to the doctor to get her eyes checked. The doctor had already scheduled her for surgery a few days later and wanted to know why she came to the office for an unscheduled visit. She said, "I want to get my eyes checked."

He replied, "You already had your eyes checked. You have cataracts, and that's why we're doing surgery on you in a few days."

She insisted, "Doctor, please just take one more look at my eyes."

He did—and was astonished. "I don't know what happened," he said, "but you don't have cataracts anymore."

She replied, "I know exactly what happened—God healed me."

In Luke 5:17-26 we read about a paralyzed man who was taken to Jesus by some friends of his. The crowd around Jesus at the house He was ministering in was so large that the man's friends couldn't get close to Him. Finally they went up to the roof, took up some tiles, cut a hole in the roof, and lowered the paralyzed man down to Jesus.

The first thing Jesus said in response was "Friend, your sins are forgiven" (v. 20). The Pharisees, a group of religious enemies of Jesus, became angry with Him, thinking, "Who does this guy Jesus think He is? Nobody can forgive sins except God!"

Jesus asked the question "Which is easier, to say, 'Your sins are forgiven,' or 'Be healed, get up, and walk'? But just to show you that I have the power to heal this man's spiritual condition, I'll deal with his physical condition as well" (vv. 21-24, author's paraphrase). And the man got up and walked away.

It was a miracle of healing—of double healing in fact. The man's body was healed, but more important, his spirit was healed. His sins were forgiven—and that was by far the greater miracle. Physical healings don't last; people eventually die. My elbow, knee, and hamstrings feel very good right now, but some day, according to the natural course of things, I'm going to die. By contrast, a spiritual healing is forever and ever. It lasts for an eternity. God wants to deal with our pain and diseases. He wants to heal our spiritual ailments. He wants to work a great miracle in every human life.

When you look at the life of Jesus, you see that the reason Jesus healed people is that He had compassion for them. He "was moved with compassion toward them, and he healed their sick" (Matt. 14:14, KJV). "Jesus had compassion on them, and touched their eyes: and immediately their eyes received sight" (Matt. 20:34, KJV). When Jesus demonstrated compassion for people, that's when the physical and spiritual deliverance started.

God has been showing me that if you're going to pray for people, if you want to see lives changed and people healed, you must have compassion for them, you have to care truly, authentically for them. That's the only way they're going to be healed, physically and spiritually.

When we pray, when we trust God, when we care about people, miracles happen. God's power intervenes on our behalf in a way that could never happen in a purely natural realm.

Adapted from Reggie White, *In the Trenches* (Nashville, Thomas Nelson, 1997). Used by permission.

Reggie White *was an all-pro tackle for the Green Bay Packers when that team won the world championship at Super Bowl XXXI. He was nicknamed "Minister of Defense." He is a graduate of the University of Tennessee, where he was an all-American football player. He founded the Inner City Church of Knoxville, Tennessee, as well as the Urban Hope Corporation of Green Bay, Wisconsin. He and his wife, Sara, have two children.*

Rob Taylor

AN AUDIENCE OF ONE

You might think that a player on a university football team that won one game in four years and then played for a National Football League team that wasn't much better would develop a loser's complex.

You would be wrong! Some guys might do that, but I certainly didn't. Because when I wasn't playing for the Northwestern University Wildcats or the Tampa Bay Buccaneers, I was playing for an audience of one—the Lord Jesus Christ.

A lot of people didn't understand it, but it's true. I was motivated to do my best for Him. Don't get me wrong—I would have loved to play for a winning team. But since I didn't, I learned to find my joy in another way. I loved defeating my opponent in the blocking scheme that a play called for. The fact is, I rarely looked at the scoreboard. I focused on my assignment. For me, winning or losing depended on how well I carried out my responsibilities on each play. If I completed my blocking assignment and dominated my man on the play, I won.

While I lived in several different cities, I spent my high school years in Dayton, Ohio. I grew up in the home of an evangelist. My dad, Rev. Bob Taylor, spent most of his life trying to convince people that they needed Jesus. He pastored a few years but spent most of his time on the road going from meeting to meeting. I usually explain to people that his work is a lot like Billy Graham's but on a much smaller scale.

As a result of Dad's calling, I spent most of my young life in church services. My mother, sister, and I often provided the special music for the services. While some of my friends may have thought I was somewhat different, I was living the life I had embraced when I was six years old and asked Jesus to come into my heart. Later, when my dad came off the road to pastor for a short time at Farmer's Branch, Texas, I experienced another defining moment in my life.

I'll never forget that night. Billy Graham was holding a crusade in what was then the new Texas Stadium. It was one of the first major events held in that stadium. Since I was a huge Dallas Cowboys fan at the time, I was more anxious about visiting the team's new home than I was about hearing Billy Graham. Much to my surprise, Tom Landry, coach of the Dallas Cowboys, and Roger Staubach, their great all-pro quarterback, shared their testimonies. I listened carefully, and at 12 years of age I determined that I wanted to be a Christian athlete. It seemed as if God sparked a fire in me and created a passion within me to be like those men of God some day. Following the service, my dad took me backstage to get the autographs of both Coach Landry and Roger Staubach, and I decided that no matter what, I was going to follow Jesus and never turn back.

My high school years were spent at Fairmont High School in Dayton, Ohio. I was an all-district and all-state tackle on the football team, so I was recruited by a number of colleges. It was quite an honor to be recruited by Ohio State, Purdue, and Northwestern University, to mention a few. I knew that I wanted to play in the Big Ten Conference. With the encouragement of my parents, my high school coach, and a member of our church, I chose Northwestern. It might sound strange to choose Northwestern over the other powerhouse football teams, but I wanted to study electrical engineering and felt that Northwestern offered the best educational opportunity in that field. I was strong in math and sciences, and education was very important to me. So after much prayer, I committed to Northwestern.

As I mentioned earlier, I learned not to look at the scoreboard. After all, putting together a record of 1-42-1 was very depressing. I focused on my responsibilities and got my pleasure from winning my private war on the offensive line. My goal became to think of a way in which God had blessed me and then to express my thanks by giving Him a "praise performance." Remember—I was playing for an audience of one.

After graduation I was drafted by the Philadelphia Eagles and went to training camp with them, but I didn't make the cut. I was then picked up by the Baltimore Colts. Again, I failed to make the team. So I went back to Ohio to wait and see what God would do.

One great thing came from my time with the Eagles. Our training camp was near Westchester, Pennsylvania. Our coach, Dick Vermeil, allowed us time off to attend church on Sunday mornings. I went to a nearby church to worship and have my soul fed. I wanted to keep my relationship with Jesus healthy. It was there that I met the love of my life, Susan. We were soon married, and we have been blessed with three wonderful children.

After being cut by the Eagles, I returned to Dayton to try to determine the course of my life. I believe the promise of Jer. 29:11—"'I know the plans I have for you,' declares the LORD. 'Plans to prosper you and not to harm you, plans to give you hope and a future.'" I believed that God had plans for me. While I didn't know what they were, I waited and prayed.

While waiting for God's plan to develop, I was contacted by Coach George Allen about playing for the newly formed United States Football League. He offered me a contract with the Chicago Blitz, I accepted, and I soon found myself playing football again. George Allen was not just a great motivator—he also attended our team chapel services and taught me a lot about life and football. Then it happened again. The league folded, and I was once more out of the game. I had learned another lesson while I was in Chicago. Walter Peyton, the all-pro running back for the Chicago Bears, gave his testimony. He said the secret of his success was training 365 days a year. After hearing that, I worked harder than ever.

When the league folded, Susan and I, along with her parents, decided to go to Largo, Florida, near Tampa. Susan's father, John Kelley, had read in the newspaper that the Tampa Bay Buccaneers were in need of an offensive lineman and suggested that I give them a call. He didn't understand that that's not the way it works in the NFL. However, because of his persistence, the day before we were to leave I decided to make that call anyway. After all, I had nothing to lose. To my surprise, I was invited to come on over if I wanted to. But I was also told that the team roster had been just about completed.

I went to the team facility, ran a few 40-yard dashes, lifted weights, and did a general workout for them. Again I was told that the team roster was just about filled up. So I returned to Pennsylvania thinking that football as I had known it was over.

I'll never forget the ringing of my phone when the Bucs called and invited me to come to training camp. I was elated. The camp experience was terrific, and I made the team as a backup offensive tackle. When Marvin Powell, the player I was backing up, was hurt in about the sixth game, I got my chance to play. God helped me, and I played that spot for Him for eight years. Again, I always did my best as I kept my focus on playing for my audience of One.

I was truly blessed. I got paid to play the game I loved. Sure, there were some incidents with non-Christian players. One of them strongly objected to my announcement of Bible studies for team members. However, I was able to maintain a strong relationship with God. I stayed spiritually healthy because I studied the Bible and had regular meetings with God and focused on knowing Christ intimately. It also helped to hold myself accountable to my Christian teammates. They knew what and whom I represented, and I was determined never to fail them.

My playing days are over now. But the joy of representing Jesus continues. I want to live in such a way that I win my battle in the game of life for Him. His grace has given me a fabulous life. It's by His grace that I've gotten this far, and it's by His grace that I live a life of joy today. And it will be by His grace that I continue to live a life of joy in the days He has planned for me.

That promise of Jer. 29:11 has truly been fulfilled in my life.

Rob Taylor *played football for Northwest University, where he earned Big 10 honors. He played for several United States Football League teams for three years and was the starting offensive tackle for the Tampa Bay Buccaneers for eight years. He and his wife, Susan, live in Tampa, Florida. They have three children.*

Gene Williams

NEIGHBORHOOD RUNT FINDS REAL JOY

I was the runt of the whole neighborhood when I was growing up. And it wasn't easy! My parents had very little education, and they worked long, tedious hours to support our family. But my dad and mom were loving and godly, and I grew up in a very happy home.

We kids gathered regularly in an empty field near our Nashville neighborhood to play ball—whatever ball was in season at the time. I was 5'2" tall and uncoordinated, and I was always the last kid chosen when the "captain of the day" picked his team. One day I struck out four times and made three errors in just one baseball game.

I remember just feeling glad that there was a "last pick." At least that meant I got to play. I did get tired of hearing "I had Gene yesterday—you have to take him today." I don't know why I wasn't deeply scarred by those days, but I wasn't.

While my family didn't enjoy any of life's luxuries, my parents gave me what really mattered—love and a wonderful example to pattern my life after. I didn't have any of the "stuff" that people think happiness is made of, and I had no athletic ability. But I had something even better—a Christian home.

Finally, between seventh and ninth grades I began to grow. By the time I started tenth grade, I was no longer the runt. I still wasn't very talented, but I worked hard and earned a spot on every sports team at East Nashville High School. The coaches didn't come looking for me to be on their teams, but during my senior year I was chosen as one of the two outstanding athletes in my school.

Unfortunately, I was so wrapped up in trying to do well in sports that I didn't spend much time hitting the books. All I wanted to do was to play ball.

Just before graduation day, God did the strangest thing. He chose me! I wasn't even last pick. He chose me to be on His team. He came looking for *me*! He didn't care that I was a poor student who failed an English class because he was too shy to make a two-minute speech in front of the class. And here's the best part: I had been having fun in life, but when God tapped me on the shoulder, my life went into joyful orbit.

While some people may struggle with their spiritual lives, I can honestly say that I never have. I was so glad to be free from the guilt of my sins that I felt like a bird that had been let out of its cage. And when He chose me to be a minister of His word, my purpose for living was defined. He gave me the opportunity to make a difference in my world. I knew why I was on earth, and I pursued His assignment as I had pursued my involvement in sports. To do that meant that I needed to continue my studies to prepare for the fulfillment of His call on my life.

There was something especially rewarding about working my way through four years of college and three years of graduate school. The Lord gave me the strength and energy to carry a full academic load and work to support myself. In fact, by the time I enrolled in seminary, I was carrying 16 hours, working 40 hours, and pastoring a small church 65 miles away on the weekends. By seminary time there were four of us—my wife, Bettye, two babies, and me. Yet in spite of the hard work, my life was full of great joy. It wasn't easy, but I was having a ball.

Sometimes I wonder if I missed something. Maybe I was supposed to have struggled with God's call to the ministry and the conditions under which we lived during those early years.

After all, it's not convenient to live in one room, share a bath, and cook on a two-burner hot plate on the back porch. But Bettye was incredibly supportive and did not complain. We had a call on our lives and an opportunity to fulfill it. No physical discomforts could take away the joy of serving Jesus.

Along the way there have been small churches (as with an attendance of 12, of which 5 were Bettye, our 3 kids, and me). There have also been churches that could not financially support us. So I not only had the joy of pastoring but also teaching high school and coaching football as well as basketball, which I thoroughly enjoyed. Working with those young men was a great joy. I was also blessed to pastor some great churches, one of which had over 2,000 members. Those churches provided good financial support for us. There were churches that had enormously talented laypersons and churches with very little talent. There were churches in the country and churches in the city. Regardless of where we were, I experienced the constant joy that came from serving Jesus. He wanted me on His team. There's no substitute for the joy of being in the center of His will.

I would like to paraphrase David's statement in Ps. 37:25—

I have been young and now I am old. Yet He has never failed to provide the necessities of life and joy beyond anything I could have ever deserved.

If by some means I could return to that neighborhood in east Nashville and be a kid starting out once again, I would leap at the chance to be on His team. I must thank our Master for His provision described in John 10:10—"I have come that they may have life, and have it to the full." He has truly given me a life filled with joy that has overflowed with His riches. It may sound strange to talk about joy in the valley, but believe me—it's possible. I have journeyed through difficult, dark days three times. On two of those occasions, someone I loved died. The other time my son survived. Each time as I walked through "the valley of the shadow of death" (Ps. 23:4), I had a special Companion who stayed by my side and assured me that He could get me through. And He did!

God has even given me joy each time I have entered the Valley of Sorrows. The first time I entered that valley was when my father, who had been my inspiration and model, went to heaven. Dad was much too young to die, but he did. A massive heart attack was his mode of transportation to heaven. He had set such a wonderful example of godliness before me that there was no question as to his eternal destiny. And while it was very painful losing him, I was happy that he was with Jesus.

That may sound like a paradox. But Dad had only a third-grade education and could not read well. He loved the Bible and wanted to know everything he could about God. So I think the Lord just decided to let him come on up to heaven for face-to-face conversations. Now he knows the answers to all of the questions he had, and I rejoice in that. How could I not find joy in his coronation?

The second time I plummeted into the valley was when one of my children didn't think life was worth living. It was a deep, dark valley—indescribable. God blessed us with four sons and a daughter, whom I love very much and to whom I've always tried to be a good father. I attended their games and yelled at the referees like any good dad, took the boys hunting and fishing, and even bought a horse for my daughter. We prayed for them and with them. So when one of my sons suddenly appeared in our bedroom with a gun and attempted suicide in front of his mother and me, the valley became as black as midnight.

Suddenly in that darkness as we waited for the ambulance, my Shepherd turned a light on. He whispered in my heart, "He's not going to die. This is war between you and Satan. You love those kids so much, and that's where you're most vulnerable." He told me two things that I desperately needed to know—the outcome and the reason.

So where is the joy? It comes from knowing and serving a God who loves and understands human beings. It's in knowing that He has the final word in this war with Satan and brings us victoriously through whatever battles we face. Joy comes from seeing our child use that "nightmare" experience years later as a high school teacher and coach to reach scores of confused young people with a message of hope.

The third trip through the valley came when Bettye, my beloved wife of 39 years, partner in ministry, and mother of my five children, was suddenly taken from me. We didn't even get to say good-bye. A massive stroke was her vehicle to heaven. How in the world can there be joy in that deep ravine of sorrow? Joy came one afternoon when my Shepherd, who remained close by my side, told me in no uncertain terms that I was going to survive. Listen to what He promises in Isa. 43:2—"When you pass through the waters, I will be with you; and when you pass through the rivers, they will not sweep over you. When you walk through the fire, you will not be burned; the flames will not set you ablaze."

Joy came in knowing that He could get me through that miserable valley. It came in the confidence that Bettye knew in full what we both believed to be true: heaven is real. I know that it sounds strange to speak of joy in the valley, but that can be a reality. David wrote, "Even though I walk through the valley of the shadow of death, I will fear no evil, for you are with me; your rod and your staff, they comfort me" (Ps. 23:4). David was not referring here to joy in sorrow. He was speaking about the confidence of survival. I want to add to this that we can experience the joy of companionship with a Shepherd who loves us very much.

Sometimes sorrowful occasions bring together people

whose lives have been headed in different directions. When that happens, the reunion is a joyful experience. Difficult experiences can make our hearts tender and result in joyful relationships.

As I journeyed through the valley, He came, touched my heart, assured me of survival, and restored joy to my heart, soul, and, in fact, my entire life. I truly found joy in the valley.

More than 50 years have come and gone since I entered the ministry, including some really tough years—but there have also been years that have provided more excitement and pleasure than I could have ever dreamed of experiencing. Praise His name!

Gene Williams *pastored for 47 years. He and his wife, Joyce, are the founding directors of Shepherds' Fold Ministries, through which they encourage and affirm pastors and their families around the world. Gene speaks in many settings in North America and internationally and has worked with numerous other ministries, including the Billy Graham Evangelistic Association. He is the author of 12 books. Gene and Joyce live in Wichita, Kansas. Between them they have seven children.*

Randy Davidson
THE LOOK

My son Cameron spent six months in the Los Angeles area with a movie studio participating in an internship program as part of his communications major. Afterward, one day he and I were talking about a movie we had watched together. As we discussed one of the actors in the movie, Cameron made the comment, "Yeah, he has the look!"

"What do you mean, 'the look'?" I asked.

"Well, he explained, "it's that special aura—his features, his personality, his smile. He just catches your attention, and he stands out in any crowd. People who have 'the look' just are special above other people."

A few years later I thought back to that conversation when I realized that "the look" applies to more than just Hollywood celebrities.

I have practiced emergency medicine for over 17 years now, and I've seen thousands of patients. In the course of my practice I've seen hundreds of patients die.

My first experience with death came during my third year as a medical student at Truman Medical Center in Kansas City. An elderly retired Baptist preacher named John Ryan was visiting me that day for a routine follow-up on his blood pressure. He was a kind, gentle man who had been a widower for a number of years. We often talked about our lives, and he told me a lot about the years he served as pastor at local churches.

Right after his checkup, on his way down the hall, John Ryan collapsed. I heard the "code blue" call and ran out into the hall to see what had happened. We started CPR on Rev. Ryan and waited for help to arrive and bring a cart so we could take him to the Emergency Room to further resuscitate him. During CPR, he opened his eyes and in his kind, gentle voice said, "No, please don't."

I clearly remember the look on his face when he said that. There was no terror, no pain, no fear. Calmness radiated from him as he smiled at me one last time and then passed on. We continued to beat on him and stick him with tubes and needles for a time, and then he was pronounced dead.

In stark contrast, I had a patient a number of years ago who came to me with severe shortness of breath and chest pain. He was a middle-aged male with end-stage emphysema. Over the course of the next few hours we tried everything we could to improve his breathing and oxygenation without success. Slowly, but surely, it became clear to us that he was not going to make it.

Unfortunately, the patient knew it too. He struggled and gasped for every last breath before he succumbed to his terminal illness. Terror, fear, and panic contorted his face and body as he faced his own mortality. He pleaded and begged for help. Sadly, we weren't prepared to give him the help he really needed. From our conversation with his family, it became apparent to me that he was not a Christian. He had no hope.

Through the years I have learned to recognize "the look." It's not sexy eyes, a perfect profile, great hair, or looks to die for. The real "look" to die for is the look of *faith*.

When I walk into the room of a critically ill or dying patient, I can tell you almost without exception if the patient is a Christian or not. The John Ryan look of peace and calmness is found only on people of faith. It's the look that comes from knowing the promise of God that if we believe in His Son, we'll be saved and have eternal life.

Probably the most heart-wrenching yet faith-building experience I've ever had began with a call from an incoming ambulance that a patient was being brought in with severe back pain, syncope (passing out), low blood pressure, and pulsatile mass in his abdomen. The patient was an 84-year-old male with a medical history that caused us to suspect a rupturing aortic aneurysm.

When the patient arrived, I examined the alert, pleasant, elderly man. His wife was at his side, stroking his forehead and firmly clasping his weathered hand in hers. Tears streamed down her face as she lovingly talked to him of their many wonderful years together. Occasionally they laughed at memories of some silly escapade from their past.

My work-up quickly confirmed my fears of the aneurysm. The patient, Mr. Thomas, was not a candidate for surgery due to other medical conditions, his age, and the medications he was taking. As I gathered the chart and information, I kept searching for a way to tell Mr. and Mrs. Thomas the prognosis. Mr. Thomas had a rupturing aneurysm, and he was going to die within the next few hours.

But when I entered the room with my news, I was relieved to see that Mr. Thomas had "the look." I could see in those light blue eyes the peace and calmness I remembered in John Ryan. I sat in a chair next to the loving couple and told them the news. When I finished, they slowly turned to look at each other with eyes that spoke of years of tenderness and care.

I quietly left the room and left them alone to spend their final hours together in privacy.

Over the next few hours I heard many comments from the nurses and aides who made periodic visits into the room to check on Mr. Thomas. There were stories of the two of them "smooching," as Mrs. Thomas called it. She was overheard telling her husband of her love and devotion to him and that she was thankful for their 60 years of marriage. Their tears were mixed with tender laughter. Mr. Thomas died with his wife cuddled up next to him in his bed, stroking his face and kissing his thin, gray hair.

This couple's faith made a strong impact on the staff who cared for them. They made sure that we all knew that they had no fears for Mr. Thomas' fate and that they knew they would be together again soon in heaven. Many of the staff members commented on "the look."

My prayer is that at the end of my life my relationship with my Lord will be reflected in a look of peace. I want to live so that His love and joy will be reflected in my life and in my face.

Randy Davidson *is a board-certified emergency medicine physician. He has served for 17 years in the emergency room at Wesley Medical Center in Wichita, Kansas. He and his wife, Laurel, live with their son, Chance, in Viola, Kansas. Their other son, Cameron, is married and lives in Fayetteville, Arkansas. Their daughter, Christy, lives in Goddard, Kansas.*

Wayne Atcheson

Dreams Do Come True

I grew up in church, and God has been a part of my life ever since I can remember. My dad was a country preacher in Alabama, and when I was little I went with him every Saturday as he preached on the streets of small Alabama towns.

My dad also held tent revivals. My commitment to Jesus Christ was made on a hot, humid night at the close of one of Daddy's stirring messages when I was eight years old. I remember walking down that sawdust trail and kneeling at the wooden altar my own daddy had built. It pleases me to say that as a boy and teenager I never rebelled against my father's passion to preach the gospel and win souls to Christ.

During those growing-up years I had two loves—Christ and sports. A typical Alabama kid, I dreamed of playing football for the Crimson Tide at the University of Alabama. More important to me than my dream, though, was the commitment I made at 14 when I promised God that I would serve Him in any way He chose to use me. The path He led me on has been different than what I would have chosen that day at summer camp, but it has been filled with great joy.

I wasn't big enough to pursue my football dreams, so I started writing about sports in high school. I worked my way through Samford University, a Christian college in Birmingham, Alabama, as sports information director. Bobby Bowden—*the* Bobby Bowden of Florida State fame—was our football coach at the time.

After graduating with a degree in journalism, I moved on to

graduate school at the University of Alabama. I served as a graduate assistant in sports information and was blessed to be there when Alabama won the national championship for the 1964-65 season. I was also privileged to work on a daily basis with the legendary Paul "Bear" Bryant for two years. As part of my work scholarship, I lived and ate with the team in the athletic dormitory and was fortunate to work with great players such as Joe Namath, Steve Sloan, and Kenny Stabler. It was a dream come true to be on the inside of big-time college football.

In September 1964 our college chapter of the Fellowship of Christian Athletes (FCA) was started. I was able to attend FCA summer camps and rubbed shoulders with notable college and professional athletes. Those experiences groomed me for success as I pursued God's will for my life.

At the age of 24 I received a letter from the national office of the FCA in Kansas City offering me a position as a full-time staff member. I had to find Kansas City on the map—it seemed so far from Alabama! But like Abraham, I was ready to follow God's leading.

For the next six years I traveled for the FCA and was involved in ministry with top Christian athletes and coaches. I'm so grateful to God for the opportunity He gave me to use my love of sports to point people to Christ.

When I was 29 I met my beautiful, Spirit-filled wife, Barbara, at an FCA camp in Estes Park, Colorado. We were married eleven months later and began our ministry together. He blessed us with our two precious daughters, Elizabeth and Amy.

Satan tried to disrupt God's plan for my life with false aspirations that seemed appealing for a time, but through God's faithfulness to me and the help of a good Christian friend, Dal Shealy, I was able to return to the arena of university athletics at the University of Richmond, in Virginia.

I had been friends with Ray Perkins during my days as a student in Alabama. Ray became head coach at the University of Alabama following Bear Bryant's death, and he called me one morning to tell me about an opportunity with the Crimson Tide. I made a quick trip to Tuscaloosa to visit with Ray and four days later was offered the job of sports information director at the university. I still consider that move as a miracle from God. I learned that when God wants to do something in our lives, He can bring it about even when it seems impossible.

For several years I was in charge of media relations for all athletics at the University of Alabama. Part of my responsibilities included distributing more than 500 credentials for each game, and I worked with ABC, NBC, CBS, and ESPN crews for televised games. During that time I became FCA advisor and met with the athletes on Wednesday nights at 9 o'clock. I also taught college Sunday School classes and was a lay speaker. It was a tremendously exciting chapter in my life.

When Coach Perkins left Alabama, I shifted to Tide Pride, the football donor program that raises millions of dollars each year through the assignment of the 42,000 choicest seats and the 85 skyboxes at the stadium. God was in control of the shifting of my responsibilities, and between 1990 and 2002 I was able to write four Christian books, including one on the history of the FCA. In 1999 I was privileged to work as executive director of the West Alabama Festival with Franklin Graham.

In 2001 I was reunited with Jerry Jenkins, coauthor of the best-selling *Left Behind* series. Jerry and I had met at an FCA camp in New York in 1972. Jerry had just purchased the Christian Writers Guild, and he asked me to consider joining his staff to promote and recruit Christian writers across the United States to be trained by the Guild to write books, stories, and articles that would glorify Christ.

Over the next two months I wrote down 50 clear signs from

the Lord that He wanted me to leave Alabama football and take the position Jerry had offered. It meant relocating to Colorado Springs. But God made His will crystal clear, so the final decision was an easy one. Once again, God opened a door and directed my path.

Even though it meant leaving Alabama, I was determined to obey the Lord regardless of the cost. Abundant blessings are the result of absolute obedience to His plan, and there's wonderful joy in carrying out His will.

God wants what's best for us. He uses life's hardships to groom us to be more like Him, and He blesses us as we journey through life with Him.

Isa. 1:19 tells us, "If you are willing and obedient, you will eat the best of the land." I know this is true, and I urge you to claim and possess your heavenly blessings in your earthly walk.

Wayne Atcheson is admissions manager of the Jerry B. Jenkins Christian Writers Guild in Colorado Springs, Colorado. He is the former University of Alabama Sports information director and was on the National Fellowship of Christian Athletes staff for 12 years. He is the author of five books. He and his wife, Barbara, have two daughters.

Ron Baldwin

JOY IN THE FACE OF DEATH

I grew up in Baxter Springs, Kansas, a small town in the southeast corner of the state famous for its giant catfish. I accepted Christ when I was eight years old, and I knew then, as I do now, that He had a plan for my life. He has never left my side, regardless of how many times I've messed up. And as the good people of Baxter Springs can testify, I was an expert at messing up.

My faith in Jesus and His presence in my life have shaped who I am and what I believe. Even the painful events of life have been faith builders and have allowed me to experience God's grace firsthand.

My life has been a privileged one. I've been blessed in business in the field of corporate banking, and I've moved steadily through the ranks—which has pleasantly surprised me and stupefied the folks of Baxter Springs. He has also blessed me with my wonderful wife, Cindy, and two great kids, a son and a daughter.

When health problems broadsided me at the age of 47, I could have been totally devastated. I wasn't, though, because God had a better idea.

It began with rashes, a persistent cough, night sweats, and difficulty swallowing pills. Since those symptoms didn't come all at the same time, I was able to rationalize that each problem was no big deal. But when an ugly lump appeared on my neck, I knew I was in trouble and that it was time to see the doctor.

Twenty-four hours later, the doctor was sitting in our living room giving us the grim news that I had lymphoma.

I knew my options were to get depressed, give up, and become bitter—or face this life-and-death challenge in His strength. I chose the latter and was determined to glorify God through my cancer.

I also decided that if friends and family were willing to walk with me on this journey, I would welcome them with open arms. Going public with my illness and allowing people to share my struggles has proved to be one of the greatest blessings of my life. Believe it or not, if we have the grace of God and the support of believing friends, we can still experience joy when staring death in the face.

A few days after the biopsy and bone marrow test, my doctor visited me once again at my home. (Yes, some doctors still make house calls.) The diagnosis, he said, was non-Hodgkin lymphoma—very serious and often fatal. There were a lot of tears that day, but I had the overwhelming feeling that God would be glorified through all that we were facing. I found some comfort in believing that I would be used to lift Him up.

The next 12 days were a whirlwind. There was an impromptu healing service in my home with 60 close friends. We received hundreds of phone calls telling us about thousands of prayers being offered on my behalf. An E-mail distribution list was developed so that we could keep my prayer partners updated. As we headed to Mayo Clinic in Rochester, Minnesota, for a second opinion, we felt the love of so many through their flowers, cards, hugs, and prayers.

Imagine our joy when the new pathology tests revealed that I did not have non-Hodgkins lymphoma but a different kind of Hodgkins disease that was very treatable. I consider it a miracle and a testimony to the power of prayer. I never thought I would celebrate Hodgkins disease, but we were thrilled. As I look back on those 12 days now, I thank God for the opportunity to have faced my own mortality in such a personal way. It changed me forever.

My experience caused me to make five major changes in my life, and I recommend these changes to you:

1. Consider each day as a new opportunity, and don't take it for granted. I don't want to miss one blessing that each new day might bring.

2. Get your finances in order. I now have the peace of mind that comes with knowing that my wife won't have to struggle with difficult business matters if something happens to me.

3. Remember that relationships are your most important asset. When you look death in the face, your wife, children, family, friends, coworkers, and prayer partners are all that really matter. I'll never underestimate the value of these relationships.

4. Take good care of your spiritual health. Scripture has new meaning to me now. Prayer is a priority. I share my faith almost daily. I live my life according to what will glorify God.

5. Learn to be a good *receiver* as well as a giver. The gifts of prayer and love and the support of my friends have brought a beautiful new dimension to my life. I expect that the lessons I have learned about receiving will equip me to better appreciate the gift Christ extended by His death on the Cross.

I have more joy in living now than I did before I heard "You have cancer." My prayer is that I never fall back into just living a good life. I want to live a *godly* life that reflects the joy of Christ.

Rob Baldwin *is president and chief operating officer of Intrust Bank in Wichita, Kansas. He has served as executive vice president with Bank of*

America and is a past president of Bank IV of Oklahoma. He serves on the National Advisory Council for the Small Business Administration Government Relations Council. He and his wife, Cindy, live in Wichita, Kansas. They have two children.

Paul Burnham

GOD'S ETERNAL PLAN

Our son Martin and his wife, Gracia, served as missionaries in the Philippines. They were captured in May 2001 and held for more than a year by Muslim extremists. Martin and Gracia were forced to live in deplorable conditions without food, water, shelter, or proper clothing. People around the world prayed for them as government forces worked to locate and free them.

My wife, Oreta, and I stayed at our home in Rose Hill, Kansas, and cared for Martin and Gracia's three children. We wanted to keep their lives as normal as possible under the circumstances, and we tried to keep them informed about what was happening while shielding them from the false stories and rumors that were circulating.

During these trying months our hope and trust were in God alone. We were encouraged by and grateful for the many prays for our family. We were grateful for the government's working to secure Martin and Gracia's release. Never did we doubt that our God is a gracious and loving God. We know He does not allow His children to suffer needlessly, but His eternal plan is to use times of suffering for the furthering of the gospel and the strengthening of faith. We took comfort in knowing that our all-wise and loving God was doing a great work and that we could trust Him to accomplish it.

Martin and Gracia were not released the way we had hoped. During the gunfight that took place in a rescue attempt, Martin was released to heaven. Gracia was rescued, though wounded, and was returned to her family.

Of course, there are things Oreta and I don't understand. Why was Martin's life taken at such a young age? Why was Gracia left to raise three children as a single mom? We confess, in our limited vision, that it's not easy to see these things as part of a good plan. But we continually find peace through putting our complete trust in God.

We have received words of encouragement from around the world. It is obvious that many people's hearts were turned toward God by Martin and Gracia's captivity. We were amazed by the number of letters that began almost the same way: "You don't know me, but this situation with Martin and Gracia has changed my life." Something else we heard over and over was "My priorities have changed—my family is more important to me now" plus "It's easier to talk about my faith to neighbors and coworkers now." People put signs in their yards, kindnesses were shown to others, and many believers were united in prayer.

God was at work. The Rose Hill schools dedicated programs to Martin and Gracia, and announcements were made regarding their faith at football games and musical programs. Many churches held special services and offered prayers for the Burnham family. Yes, Martin and Gracia's long captivity was used to further God's plan of redeeming the lost. This strengthening of the faith of so many helped us find peace and hope.

Throughout our long ordeal, Oreta and I planned to return to the Philippines some day. After Gracia's return home, and when she and her children were adjusted and doing well, we began making plans to return to the Lord's work there.

Upon our arrival in the Philippines in November 2002, it was apparent that Martin and Gracia's captivity had impacted Filipinos as well. They were relieved that we were not bitter toward the country and that we were willing to return. Many of our Filipino friends had suffered along with us. Our time with them brought healing as we shared our mutual sorrow and loss.

A Christian businessman wrote an hour-long drama starting with God creating the world and moving to Christ's redeeming work on the Cross and then on to faithful followers of Christ. Martin and Gracia's life and captivity make up a large portion of the work. It's a moving and challenging dramatization that has led many to dedicate their lives to proclaiming the gospel to their families, neighbors, and coworkers. The joy of the Lord filled our hearts as many accepted calls to serve as full-time missionaries or in pastoral ministry.

Although there was great pain and sorrow during and since this ordeal, our faith never faltered. Yes, we wish the outcome had been different and that Martin had been returned to us, but we have the calm assurance that we can count it all joy when we encounter difficulties. We're assured that God has a greater plan than just our temporary comfort.

God's plan overshadows our temporary loss. Even in our grief, we rejoice with Martin—he has attained his reward.

Some day when our time here is complete, Martin will be waiting to greet us. I can visualize his huge grin and the twinkle in his eyes. As we're reunited to spend eternity together, we'll rejoice that God's eternal plan far surpasses our imaginations.

Paul Burnham *has been married to Oreta since 1958. They have been missionaries with New Tribes Mission since 1968 and have served with a church-planting ministry among the Ibaloi Tribe in the Philippines since 1970. Four of their five children, along with their spouses, became missionaries with New Tribes Mission.*

Andy Eby
From Defeat to Victory

Approach the huddle. It's a new play. Forget the last play—put it behind you. Focus on the upcoming one. Have a short memory. You can't live on the glory or the failure of the past play. Once in the huddle, tune out the distractions. Talk to the other players. Focus on the quarterback. He calls the play. He breaks the huddle. Run to the line of scrimmage. As the center, make the offensive line calls. Look at the defense—read what they're trying to do. Make calls to the others on the line. Stay ready, and wait for the quarterback to make his cadence. Focus on him. Hike! Make the best block possible. Keep the opponent from making his play. Run the best play possible so the ball carrier can reach his goal. End of play. Back to the huddle.

Same old routine. Huddle . . . call the play . . . end of play . . . huddle. It's like a bunch of little games in one big game, and distractions are all around. No one else is responsible for blocking out the distractions and making the plays happen, regardless of how the team is performing as a whole. Yet it's about the team and for the team. The goal is to win the game. Right?

For me, playing football became routine. I just went through the motions. I made the smallest investment of myself I could make to complete the plays successfully. I got by, but I didn't enjoy it. In fact, I hated it. I grew more and more miserable, and I dreaded every day. My hope was fixed on the time when I wouldn't play football anymore and all of this would go away.

To my dismay, I was in the same place spiritually that I was in football. I was raised as a Christian, and I went to church every Sunday. I was a "good kid," and my friends knew I didn't do the so-called "bad things." As far as I was concerned, being a Christian meant that there were a lot of things I *couldn't* do. I couldn't drink, couldn't smoke, couldn't party, couldn't have sex. That was it. I was just going through the motions. It was frustrating to be a Christian when my life didn't seem different from anyone else's. I knew I was going to heaven, but I wasn't experiencing the goodness and joy that God has for us on earth. I certainly wasn't living in victory.

I had no passion, no force inside to draw people to me. I knew I either needed to quit football or change my outlook and actions to reflect Christ more.

I asked God to remove me from the situation, because surely a Christian isn't supposed to be so miserable. I figured I must be in the wrong spot. Then I noticed that everyone around me (in my football world) suffered with the same struggles and pressure to perform. It hit me that I needed to stay since my problems wouldn't go away simply by quitting football. My problems would follow me wherever I went.

I knew that I needed to change to survive and that I needed to open my life to God and allow Him to use me right where I was. I had to begin to make a difference—to *be* different. I began to seek the Lord in everything. I became hungry for the truth of God, and the Lord gave me a passion to know Him more. I had to find joy in my life.

God showed me that I was focusing on the mountains in front of me rather than on the Mountain *Mover*. I began to shift the focus off my situation and onto God, others, and my mission to love Him more. For the first time in my life, I learned about the power of the Cross. I had been well schooled in religion, and I knew what Christ did for me on the Cross. But there's a distinction between *knowing* God's word and *experiencing* it. It finally began making sense. Jesus didn't die on the

Cross and carry the weight of the world on His shoulders so I could walk in defeat and depression. He died to free me from the chains of this world. I realized I could experience freedom here on earth and that I didn't have to wait for heaven to know the power of His sacrifice! God wants me to experience that great joy *now*.

When that truth came alive in me, I became more ruthless in my pursuit of experiencing God's freedom. My favorite story in the Bible is the Book of Joshua. When God told Joshua to lead the Israelites into the Promised Land, He said, "Now then, you and all these people, get ready to cross the Jordan River into the land I am about to give to them—to the Israelites. I will give you every place where you set your foot, as I promised Moses" (1:2-3).

God had already given Joshua victory over the people he was about to fight. I love that. What confidence Joshua must have had! He knew that no matter what the situation appeared to be, no matter what the size of the army, God said he would be the victor.

That same promise was given to me. When Jesus died on the Cross, He gave me access to the same confidence. There is no power, no person, no boss, no coach, and no situation that has power over me. Christ has given me the victory, and no person can thwart the plans of the Lord. It's awesome to know that God is in control of every situation—even the ones that seem unfair, frustrating, and painful.

Understanding this victory has freed me to experience all the blessings God has for me on this earth. I'm different now. My God has already conquered this world. There's joy in knowing that. When I accepted that truth, I began *bearing* fruit instead of *burying* it.

Before I came to this realization, I continuously tried to pump myself up and get motivated for a game by listening to fast, upbeat music and by watching movie clips or past game films. But that motivation was short-lived. Once I hit the field and started playing, I forgot about those "inspirational" tactics.

So I turned to what now motivates me: worship; honoring and focusing on God; Christian music; prayer; scripture (Ps. 18 will get you pumped up for anything!). These things stay with me after I get to the field, because they live in my heart.

So *now*—approach the huddle. Tune out the distractions. Eyes on the quarterback. Listen to his words. His plans become mine. Repeat them to the line. And remember:

> You, O LORD, keep my lamp burning; my God turns my darkness into light. With your help I can advance against a troop; with my God I can scale a wall. As for God, his way is perfect; the word of the LORD is flawless. He is a shield for all who take refuge in him. For who is God besides the LORD? And who is the Rock except our God? It is God who arms me with strength and makes my way perfect. He makes my feet like the feet of a deer; he enables me to stand on the heights. He trains my hands for battle; my arms can bend a bow of bronze. You give me your shield of victory, and your right hand sustains me; you stoop down to make me great (*Ps. 18:28-35*).

Andy Eby *is currently playing center for the St. Louis Rams. He aspires to glorify God in every aspect of his life. Andy excelled in academics as well as sports throughout his high school career and at Kansas State University. He lives in St. Louis.*

Thomas Etheredge

THE WINDING TRAIL TO THE PRAIRIE ROSE

Sitting in a hot, miserable jail cell, my thoughts drifted back . . .

My earliest memories are those of being a cowboy. When I was four or five years old, my standard wearing apparel consisted of scuff-toed cowboy boots, jeans with knee patches, and a checkered shirt with imitation pearl snaps, all topped off by a red felt cowboy hat. And I always had a horse. When I was too young for a real horse, I rode Pete, my favorite wooden horse on springs. He bounced many trails with me.

I grew up in a family who had raised and worked cattle in south Texas for generations. As a child, I was never interested in playing ball or taking part in other athletic endeavors. All my spare time and attention were devoted to *business*.

One year for Christmas I asked for a printing press so I could start a neighborhood gazette and sell it to the neighbors. I started a local weather station when I was seven years old. One spring I sold guppies to my friends for their aquariums, and when the guppies turned into frogs in the summer, I resold them to folks who wanted to keep the bugs out of their gardens.

My family went to church regularly, and church activities were an important part of my life. But somehow I missed developing a personal relationship with Jesus. Instead, I focused on business—even at church. Each Mother's Day, I could be found standing outside the educational wing of the church selling corsages to men who had forgotten to buy one in advance for their wives and mothers.

I was 11 years old when I got my first paper route. I peddled papers on the poor side of town, and early on I learned the bartering system. Just about each one of my potential newspaper customers had something to trade—often a car that was broken down in the driveway. I started trading newspaper subscriptions for broken-down cars.

My dad was a gifted mechanic. He loved me, and he loved working with me in the shop. Together we dragged the cars and motorcycles home.

One by one, we put the cars and motorcycles into working order. Before I was even old enough to drive myself, I sold cars and motorcycles to folks all over town. My bank account began to grow.

Through my preteen and teenage years and on into college, all I thought about was making business deals that I could turn into money in my pocket. I had the Midas touch. I was independent and self-sufficient, believing I could always provide for myself. From time to time God knocked on the door of my heart, but I couldn't imagine surrendering my will to His.

On April 1, 1984, I was working in my office in the Diamond Shamrock Towers in downtown Dallas. I was still a cowboy and owned a ranch in the Texas panhandle. I also owned majority shares of an investment banking company. After college, I had focused on oil and drilling for oil. I made a small fortune fixing up used drilling rigs and then selling or renting them to large exploration companies that were desperate in the late 70s and early 80s for drilling rigs. I was wheeling and dealing Texas style—doing big business by the time I was 21. By 1984 I had sold my oil and drilling companies and put everything in investments and banking.

That morning I was reading the *Wall Street Journal* and preparing to travel from Dallas to my London office. I took those Trans-Atlantic flights weekly from Dallas to London. My wife and I had three small children. I loved my family, but business was always my top priority. I reasoned that my hectic schedule was just a short-term thing and that I would soon retire and change my focus to my family.

My secretary buzzed me and told me that some Securities and Exchange Commission (SEC) agents were in the lobby wanting to see me. I remember arrogantly telling her that I wasn't seeing anyone who didn't have an appointment. A few minutes later she buzzed me again and told me that they insisted on seeing me immediately.

After they were ushered into my office, I spent the next couple of hours learning that I was facing a lengthy indictment for security violations that revolved around the merchant banking activities and investments with which my company was involved. I answered the agents' questions that morning, and after they left, I called our firm's securities attorneys in Washington, D.C. I was told that there was no problem and that our legal experts would take care of it.

I now refer to that April 1, 1984, as April Fool's Day. I flew to my home in London and stayed in constant contact with our attorneys in Washington, who had advised me to stay out of the country until the legal issues were resolved. Weeks turned into months. My family remained in Texas and was under enormous pressure. My problems were featured in the newspapers and television news almost daily. One day my London office was contacted by Scotland Yard and Interpol regarding the SEC indictments that were handed down in the United States.

Following my attorney's directions, I traveled through Europe to my Hong Kong office, then on to Singapore and later Africa. Later that year I moved to Central America and established an aloe vera plantation. I also built a processing plant where we processed the aloe into products for pharmaceutical, cosmetic, and industrial usage. The only positive event during that time was that I was reunited with my family on our plantation in the jungles of Belize.

In November we left on a business trip to Canada to sell aloe to a large cosmetic firm. That night I was notified that the very day my family and I flew out of Belize, a secret squad of Texas agents had raided our plantation. Safe in Canada, we had nothing but what we had packed for the trip. With my wife and three children there, I paced back and forth in the Canadian hotel room wondering what to do next. I continued sending cables and telegrams and making phone calls to my attorneys in Washington, only to be told to just hold on—they were working on things.

During the months that followed, I created some businesses in Canada that enabled me to make a living. I bought a partnership in a small medical weight reduction clinic, and in a few months it expanded into several locations. We were able to have a beautiful home on the outskirts of Vancouver and settled into some degree of normalcy. By Christmas of 1984 we were Canadians.

By 1985 I was wanted by the American authorities as well as by Scotland Yard, Interpol, and the Canadian Mounties. I decided to return to Texas to try to resolve my problems, and I accepted extradition. I was committed to proving my innocence, but I ended up in a stiflingly hot Texas jail cell.

Life seemed hopeless. If convicted of everything I was charged with, I faced more than 1,000 years behind bars. By now I had lost my wife and family, my houses, my automobiles, my airplane, my reputation, and my businesses. I had nothing. I was in a deep pit of despair. Although I was innocent, no one wanted anything to do with me. It seems that everyone believed I was guilty. At one time I had employees around the world at my beck and call. Now not one of them would even so much as accept a collect call from me.

At my lowest point, the jail cell door clanged open, and a man shouted "Howdy!" in a cheerful voice. He was a member of The Gideons International, a group of Christian businessmen who share the gospel by distributing God's Word. He had been by to see me previously, but this Sunday was different. He had been allowed to bring me a used Bible. It was a sad-looking book without a cover, but to me it was precious. I spent 30 wonderful minutes with my Gideon friend, and afterward I spent hours reading the Word of God that had been left with me.

For the first time in my life I realized I was helpless to do anything for myself and my family. My self-sufficiency could do nothing to help me now. Finally I fell onto my face in that concrete cell and gave my life to Jesus. I repented of my sins and called out to Him to help me. I poured out my misery to Him, confessing my sins and laying my overwhelming circumstances at His feet. I poured out the hurt of losing my family and of not being able to see my babies grow up.

Hours later as a new day dawned and the sun appeared through those prison bars, a new day dawned on my life as well. I was a new man. I wasn't dependent just on myself—my life now belonged to Jesus. I trusted Him with everything from that moment on.

As the days passed, I spent all my time reading my ragged Bible and praying. I was still facing the same issues that had put me in prison. Jesus didn't take the problems away—but He was with me in that dark valley of hopelessness. He came with me down every trail when no one else would.

By early 1989 it was over. I had faced many court hearings and had won all but one. I had served three miserable years in prison. I finally pled no contest to the last charge simply because I had no more money and no more will to fight.

As I was preparing for my release in 1989, a lady I had met through a prison ministry became very special to me. I knew

God had answered my prayers, and she became the love of my life. We were married after a short courtship.

I started over again with nothing. Cheryl and I began building a new life with Jesus at the center. Many people thought it would be impossible to crawl out of the hole I was in. But God gave me a promise in my Bible: "Return to the stronghold, You prisoners of hope. Even today I declare That I will restore double to you" (Zech. 9:12, NKJV).

I returned with Cheryl to my ranching roots to start anew. We worked long hours and ultimately purchased 40 acres and built a modest home. Every year we purchased more land and improved our cattle operation. I had always been a cowboy, so to me having a ranch was really living! God has restored my relationship with my three children from my first marriage, and in 1992 Cheryl and I were blessed with a beautiful baby girl.

In 1999 we acted upon a dream that came to us as we struggled to "think outside the box" in an attempt to improve our cattle and ranching operation. The idea was to start a chuckwagon supper. Before the first clod of earth was turned to construct the first building, Cheryl and I knelt and prayed over the dream and the venture.

Years have passed since we began the Prairie Rose Chuckwagon Supper near Wichita, Kansas, and it's now one of the state's fastest-growing tourist attractions. In 2003 more than 60,000 guests from around the world and every state in the union visited the Prairie Rose. We introduce our guests to fine western hospitality, dining, and music. With God's help we provide a great family experience. There are three theaters, the Hopalong Cassidy National Museum, an Indian village, wagon rides, train rides, a working woodworking/metalworking shop, a saddle shop, a chapel, a recreational vehicle park, and more. The Prairie Rose has grown beyond our wildest expectations.

As Cheryl and I look back, we're filled with awe at the adventure God has provided. We started with nothing but our faith in Jesus and our love for Him, and He has been faithful to us. I found true success in that hot Texas jail cell the day I gave my life to Jesus and began living for Him.

Thomas Etheredge *is a cowboy and entrepreneur. He is the founder and owner of the Prairie Rose Ranch in Benton, Kansas, which has rapidly grown to be one of the largest tourist attractions in the state. He and his wife, Cheryl, live in Benton. He is the father of four children.*

Larry Garcia

THE JOY OF THE LORD IS A CONSUMING FIRE

My family wasn't blessed with many material possessions when I was growing up, but I remember my mother praying for us and asking God to meet our needs. She prayed for our care and comfort when we couldn't be with her. All six of us children enjoyed it when our mother read the Bible to us. She taught us to respect and accept others and to treat everyone kindly. She and her parents lived their faith daily, and they were great examples to me of the importance of Jesus in my life.

I didn't know my father's parents, but he told of his grandmother tearfully bidding him goodbye and wishing him Godspeed as he was leaving Sal Tillo, Mexico, to come to the United States.

My mother's parents never failed to extend kindness to someone in need. Although they didn't have much, they generously gave to transients, hitchhikers, and neighbors. They raised cattle, hogs, and all kinds of fowl and had the largest gardens I ever saw. They were generous with gifts of meat, fresh fruits, vegetables, and canned or preserved food that they shared with their four daughters' families. It seemed that the more they gave away, the more they had to give.

I remember my grandmother reading the Bible at the end of the day. I thought at the time that she read out loud because she was hard of hearing, but now I believe she did it so that everyone who heard her would be blessed by those words.

My mother died in childbirth when I was 14. I had prayed

for her during that difficult pregnancy, but she died during the summer. I remember thinking that a really loving God wouldn't allow such a terrible thing to happen and was angry with Him for "taking" her.

My four brothers and I were fortunate to have our sister, who had just graduated from high school. She took care of the house and cooked for us.

In the fall, I had a new homeroom teacher, Mrs. Newell. She did not tolerate academic mediocrity from any of her students. And she had the audacity to focus on the feeble, listless efforts I put forth in the classroom. She was also our class sponsor, which meant that she was constantly nosing into my business—including my social life.

Mrs. Newell seemed to be everywhere I turned. As my English teacher, she required me to read books and then write reports. I remember one time I "borrowed" a classmate's book report and copied it verbatim. That was a bad mistake! Mrs. Newell kept me after class and really let me have it for committing a "deceitful act of plagiarism." She warned me to never do it again—and then went on to express her belief that I could become an honor student if I tried. She put her arm around my shoulders and said with deep compassion, "You're not the only person who lost a mother." Those words changed me and have echoed throughout my life. She helped me become a real man. It's a blessing to reflect on the various people God put into my life who made such a difference. Mrs. Newell was certainly a blessing to me.

When I graduated from high school at the age of 17, I couldn't wait to join the United States Marines Corps. I was a spoiled, selfish, and arrogant boy, and joining the Marines was probably the best thing that could have happened to me. When I left for basic training, it was the first time I had ever been outside of the state of Kansas. In the 1950s the Marines tried to break your spirit in every way and remold your character and personality with a different set of values.

I conformed to the Corps' will and ways and was a successful Marine. I spent a year in Korea and two years on the West Coast dabbling in just about every carnal experience known to humanity. I was bent on destruction even though I knew the things I was doing were against the teachings of Christ. I was honorably discharged from the Marine Corps as a sergeant in December 1956.

During the time I served in the Marines, each time I came home on leave my grandmother admonished me to seek a relationship with Jesus Christ. She also told me that it was my mother would have wanted me to do. Thank God—she took my mother's place in writing to me and encouraging me to be mindful of my upbringing. She continuously reminded me to "Seek ye the LORD while he may be found" (Isa. 55:6, KJV).

Six months after my discharge, I had used up most of my savings and finally began looking for a job. One morning as I was on my way to fill out an application, I noticed a large plume of smoke and curiously headed toward it. I parked my car about 100 feet away from a large two-story house with flames shooting from the back. Before I realized it, I was blocked in by fire trucks, with fire hoses snaking all around me.

Most of the firefighters hurried to the back of the house. Suddenly bystanders began to yell that a lady was trying to come out the front door. She seemed calm, but it was obvious that she couldn't get the screen door open. I asked her to stand back, and I stuck my foot through the screen and then reached down and unlatched the door. I led her down the steps and into the street in front of her house. News reporters gathered around me and asked why I had helped her at possible risk to myself. I answered that I hadn't considered it to be a risk. It wasn't really a *rescue*—I had simply helped her get the screen door open, and she had calmly walked out of the house.

The fire chief had driven up and was waiting to talk with me. He noticed my Marine fatigues and spit-shined boots, and after a few questions he discovered that I was looking for a job. He said, "We're not hiring firefighters right now, but if you'll take my card to the personnel office and tell them I sent you, they'll let you fill out an application." I did that, and I was hired a short time later, in June 1957.

God brought Carolyn into my life, and we were married the following February. Our marriage was blessed with two beautiful children. Although we were very happy, we were unable to find real direction for our lives.

In March 1973, Carolyn was saved and joined a church. After considerable soul searching, I also accepted Christ as my personal savior. However, I continued to struggle spiritually. Finally, I obeyed the Holy Spirit's clear message: *You need to learn about the will and way of Jesus Christ.* I began devouring the Word.

About that same time I began working to develop the Equal Employment Opportunity and Affirmative Action programs for the city of Wichita, Kansas. I became so engrossed in that work that I lost my enthusiasm for studying God's Word. Additionally, my personal ambitions were focused on becoming fire chief —but I wasn't selected because I didn't have a college degree. The rejection devastated me. I still hadn't learned the meaning of "Seek ye first the kingdom of God, and his righteousness" (Matt. 6:33, KJV).

I became consumed with completion of my degree, and for the next few years I studied hard. I finally completed my associate degree in 1987 and was soon appointed fire chief, the position I had wanted so badly. When I received the phone call asking if I was prepared to assume the duties of fire chief, I hung up the phone, closed my office door, fell to my knees, and thanked God.

Almost from the first day of my appointment, I've been given opportunities to share Christ with troubled men and women. I've talked with members of the fire service about marital infidelity, domestic violence, divorce, custody battles, substance abuse, uncontrolled anger, and many other topics. The Lord has given me scriptures that have helped me boldly proclaim the good news of Jesus Christ to the hurting people around me.

I regret that I did not embrace the teaching of my mother, my grandparents, and Mrs. Newell earlier in my life. But I finally learned that true joy comes from serving Jesus.

I've spent most of my adult life putting out fires. But I'm determined that by His grace the fire of my faith will never be extinguished and will continue to spread to those around me.

Larry Garcia *is chief of the City of Wichita (Kansas) Fire Department, where he has served since 1957. He has received many awards and has held numerous positions in the International Association of Fire Chiefs Organization. He and his wife, Caroline, have two children. They live in Wichita.*

Everett C. Hayes

JOY IN UNIFORM

My plan for my life was to become a professional photographer—despite the fact that my color vision was impaired. I was in the Navy at the time, and even though I was a Christian, I had no peace and no joy.

One afternoon while at sea, I felt God speak to me about ministering to His people. That was something I simply did not want to do. But I couldn't escape His call. After a lot of prayer, I decided to follow His leading, get out of the Navy, and go to college.

While I was in college preparing for pastoral ministry, God began to deal with me about becoming a chaplain in the military. That meant going to seminary. I had never intended to go to college, much less seminary. But I followed His leading and in a few short years had finished college and seminary and received my ordination. In 1986 I was back on active duty serving as a chaplain. Thus began a whole new chapter of my life.

My work as a chaplain was interesting—and sometimes difficult. Training required me to spend a lot of time away from my wife and two small sons as I learned how to survive. More importantly, though, I learned about the lives of the soldiers I served with. I did my best to go to every battery and every howitzer each day. I remember one exercise in which I put more than 600 miles on my jeep as I traveled around to see my people. I spent days with the hot sun bearing down on me and days standing in mud with rain pouring down on me. But because of the joy God had put in my heart, I was always able to look each soldier in the eye and smile.

I spent three years in Germany with an air defense unit, during which I spent considerable time in the field. My faith was tested when a young lieutenant who had a vibrant Christian faith was killed in an accident. I had just arrived in the field that Sunday morning to provide a worship service for the soldiers when I received a radio message from the battalion commander to report to a different location immediately. My assistant and I quickly responded to that request and learned of her death upon our arrival. The other soldiers in her unit had not yet been told. We gathered the unit together while the executive officer told his troops about the accident. I was able to step in and pray with and for those soldiers. My heart was grieving as well for this young lieutenant, and I shared my faith in Jesus Christ.

Just a couple of weeks prior to the lieutenant's death, I had visited with her at another field site. We had stood out in the pouring rain as she shared her heart and her concern for her soldiers. Now I was to conduct a memorial service for her—on the day that was to have been the day of her promotion. During her memorial service, several of the soldiers spoke about her impact on their lives, and I shared about the grace and love of Christ for just such a time as this. I closed the service by talking about the joy this young lady had found in serving Christ wherever she was and about her upcoming promotion. My closing thought was "Well done, good and faithful servant. Welcome home." Even with the pain I felt, I found joy in knowing that her life had made a difference in the lives of the soldiers she led.

Many times during my career as a chaplain I've talked to soldiers about the death of loved ones. I've had to go with a commander to a soldier's home to inform the spouse that his or her loved one wouldn't be coming home. This aspect of my calling was never easy, but God never failed to supply the strength I needed in order to minister to the needs of another.

In the heat of Somalia, where I had the joy of preaching an

Easter sunrise service; in Haiti, where I held Christmas services; in Korea, where I pastored the Protestant worship service. In every assignment, I've found great joy in serving my Lord.

Of course, I shared many birthdays, anniversaries, holidays, ball games, and other significant events only through the photographs that were sent to me. And although I would rather have been there for my family, God always provided for the needs of my wife and children.

Yes, there has been joy in my life even as I've stood in mud up to my knees. When soldiers have asked me why their prayers for better weather weren't answered, I always reply, "I'm in sales—weather is management."

Even in the midst of disappointments and sorrow, I've had a deep, abiding joy in my soul. I've never felt like throwing up my hands and giving up.

I firmly believe that God is in control. My joy overflows each time I'm reminded of His care for me and the confidence I have in Him to meet my needs until the day I meet Him face-to-face.

Everett C. Hayes *worked for more than 33 years in the military. He served as a full-time chaplain for 16 years and attained the rank of major. He and his wife, Annette, live in Junction City, Kansas. They have two sons.*

Kong Hee
The Joy of Winning the Lost

I was in my hotel room on Waikiki Beach in Honolulu in February 1995 when the strong presence of God came upon me and moved me to read Matt. 22:36-40. I read and meditated on this passage for more than an hour. As I did so, the Holy Spirit began working powerfully in my heart, revealing to me that Christianity in its simplest essence has one basic theme: Love God wholeheartedly, and love people fervently. I do love God with all my heart, and I do love people.

That evening I reflected on the years since I was saved during the early days of the Holy Spirit renewal in Singapore in 1975. For the following 13 years I worshiped in a small Anglican parish and felt that God was calling me to become an Anglican priest. However, in 1989, after being caught up in a church conflict, I became disillusioned with church politics and decided to become a missionary to the Philippines. But that was not to be.

In 1989 approximately 20 teenagers asked me to be their Bible study teacher. I agreed. So on May 7, 1989, my wife, Sun, and I founded City Harvest Church. Soon that group of 20 grew to 1,300. Despite my inexperience and foolish zeal, people just kept getting saved! I believe it was because the church was in genuine revival and that God was working for us. I can't express my joy in knowing that God was using me—*even me*—for His purposes.

Our people grew strong in prayer and spiritual warfare and deliverance. And although our church was known all over southeast Asia as a ministry with strong, radical Christians, Sun and I sensed that something was amiss. No matter what we did, the church simply would not grow any further.

But that night in Hawaii God very clearly spoke to my heart that from that point forward everything we did in City Harvest Church should be based on the two principles of loving God and loving people. I felt He was telling me that if we followed those principles, our church would grow beyond our dreams.

Armed with this revelation, I returned home and ruthlessly evaluated all our church programs. Sun and I immediately discarded programs that did not fit those two aims of loving God and people.

We began to focus on the lost during our prayer meetings. The songs we sang started to focus on the lost. Everything we did became focused on the lost. Gradually, the spiritual atmosphere of the church began to change as a sense of destiny, purpose, and faith surged through our people.

I discovered that many of our members—including church workers—simply did not know how to share the gospel with nonbelievers. We began to teach everyone the basics of soul winning. The church also took up new challenges to reach out to the poor, the elderly, the AIDS-inflicted, the street kids, the handicapped, and the disadvantaged. We were determined to find a hurt and heal it and find a need and meet it.

God wants to work with us. Mark 16:20 says that Jesus' disciples "went out and preached everywhere, the Lord working with them and confirming the word through the accompanying signs" (NKJV). No experience in life compares with working *with* God.

Since that revelation, the Lord has been working mightily among the people in our church, and roughly 2,000 new members have been added each year. Today 72 percent of the people in our congregation are first-generation, first-pastor converts.

Relatively few are transfers from other churches. City Harvest Church in Singapore started 14 years ago with a handful of people, and today it's one of the largest congregations in southeast Asia and a model for effective evangelism.

Through loving, radical, friendship evangelism, City Harvest Church has become a strong presence in its society. Both young and old attend our services. Our 15,000-member congregation meets in a new building where we hold at least 17 services each weekend. The people worship enthusiastically. When the invitation for salvation is given, hundreds of people stream toward the front to be led in the sinner's prayer.

Through the grace of God, our church has grown and navigated to the cutting edge of soul winning. The basic tenet of our ministry remains the importance of loving God wholeheartedly and loving people fervently. Sun and I and our staff and church members cannot fully express the incredible joy that comes from following that principle to win the lost to Christ.

I continue to thank God for His revelation on that beach in Hawaii. Our hearts swell with the joy of the Lord as He leads us to spread the Good News from shore to shore and around the world.

Kong Hee *was a successful businessman before entering the ministry. He and his wife, Yeow Sun, founded City Harvest Church, one of the fastest growing churches in southeast Asia. They live in Singapore.*

H. B. London Jr.

WHAT A GREAT NAME!

The first time someone called me "Pastor," it sounded strange. I felt too young to carry that title, and I also didn't feel worthy or ready for the responsibilities that accompanied that God-ordained office. (See Eph. 4:11.) But I grew to love the title, and to this day I respond to it with joy.

Pastor,

Thanks for the sermon.

My mom just died.

We're going to have a baby.

The X-rays don't look good—could you pray with me?

Thanks for being there when I needed you.

The list is endless. But you know what I mean. Whenever the phone rings or there's a knock at my office door or I read a letter, I'm ushered into a unique collection of men and women whom I have been given the privilege to shepherd. God has given me a very special opportunity that has produced abounding joy.

As a result of that call, I have had a unique relationship with my congregations. I can't remember exactly when it was, but it had to be more than 25 years ago that I stood before my church family and said, "God loves you as though you were the only person in the world to love. If He had not sent His only Son to die for the whole human race, He would have sent Him to die just for you. That makes you a very important person. And I love you too."

Probably that one phrase has been quoted by more members

of the congregations I've served than any other. I've often taken a moment before the prayer time in a morning worship service to tell my people how honored I felt to be their pastor. I've thanked them for their patience with me. I valued their comments, learned from their constructive criticism, and swelled a bit too much because of their affirmation. Through the more than three decades that I was called "Pastor," I attempted to have a love affair with my people.

I tried never to allow the business of the church to become an us-against-them situation. I always believed that it was their church. They prayed for it, sacrificed to see it born, and held steady in times of uncertain transition. I had not come there to straighten out their uncertainties but to be their pastor and to love them in the relationship they had with the living God.

"Pastor" is a beautiful word, and what a relationship it represents! Next to "Honey" or "Dad," I believe it's the most wonderful word in the English language.

Occasionally someone still calls me Pastor, and I'm still awestruck after all these years. I still feel honored and amazed. I square my shoulders and renew my purpose. I feel humbled and grateful, for there is no higher privilege than that of being called "Pastor."

God's will for my life has provided more joy than I ever dreamed of experiencing. Problems? Absolutely! But joy so far surpassed the difficulties that I would pursue His will all over in a heartbeat just for the joy that comes from following Him.

I want to be like Jesus, who, according to Heb. 12:2, "for the joy set before him endured the cross, scorning its shame, and sat down at the right hand of the throne of God." Certainly there have been some crosses to be carried and some difficulties to overcome. But the pleasure of God's presence has produced overwhelming joy and satisfaction in my life.

As a result of the call of God upon my life and the path upon which He has led me, I have experienced abounding joy in my life.

H. B. London Jr. *is a veteran pastor and for the past decade has served as a pastor to pastors around the world. He is vice president of Focus on the Family and leads the Division of Church Clergy and Medical Ministries. He is the author of numerous books. He and his wife, Beverley, live in Colorado Springs.*

Randy MacDonald
The Clear and Perfect Day— Almost

Bakersfield, California. It's a Friday morning in March 2001. I'm standing on Pit Road in front of our race truck, talking with another competitor, Jonathan, who's hoping to make his first start in the NASCAR Craftsman Truck Series. He has traveled all the way from New York. He has never raced a truck, never raced at this level in the sport, and never seen the Mesa Marin race truck until he walked through the gate this morning.

I've been to Bakersfield previously. I've been racing with the truck series since 1996. And in the previous season we finished sixth at Daytona, competed in every event during the season, and finished in the top 20 in points.

I could see that Jonathan was anxious and somewhat nervous. He would have to give the racing performance of his career. On the other hand, I wasn't at all concerned about my chances to win. In fact, I wouldn't even be racing my truck this weekend since I was still recovering from an accident from just a month earlier.

That accident happened at Daytona Speedway just two days before the tragic one that took the life of racing champion Dale Earnhardt. In fact, both wrecks not only occurred at the same track the same weekend but also happened on the same part of the racetrack.

The NASCAR community was still in shock. The danger of our sport could no longer be downplayed or ignored. Everyone knew that things had changed forever.

In my case, just 28 laps into our race at Daytona, a rookie competitor broke loose just in front of my truck. I saw him spin, and then the nose of his truck hooded the apron. As I stayed high to clear him, his truck snapped off the bottom of the track and streaked up the banking in front of me. At 187 miles per hour, you don't slow down very fast no matter how hard you use the brakes—until you hit something!

So I was at Bakersfield fully aware of the situation with my neck, knowing that I might never race again. And if I didn't have surgery now, I would have to have it later. My arms felt as if they were asleep. The bottoms of my feet burned when I lay down at night. I could feel the weight of my head. My neck could hardly hold it if I moved too fast or turned or bent.

My doctor had instructed me to wear a foam-type neck support. That doesn't look so good for a driver to wear at a racetrack, and I didn't want anyone to know about the seriousness of the injury—so I didn't wear it.

As I continued to listen to Jonathan discuss his ambitions and hopes for the race, he alluded to his concerns as well. Then I was completely taken aback when he pulled from his pocket three smooth stones that he explained were his good luck charms. One was for safe travel (he didn't like to fly), and another was for good fortune (he needed a good finish). I never did get what the third stone was for. My mind was racing about his approach to life and racing.

Spiritually speaking, I was still celebrating being able to witness to a young lady at Atlanta Motor Speedway the previous weekend. As the Winston Cup cars came off the fourth turn to take the green flag, my sister and I were in the stairway praying with that woman as she made a decision for the Lord. So Jonathan's approach was strange to me.

I asked him, "Jonathan, don't you believe in God?"

Of course, the answer to the question was a most predictable "Yes."

Then I responded, "Well, who is God? Is He the one who created the heavens and the earth? Did He create you and me? Or is He the one we created from storybooks, tradition, the influence of others, and wishful, even imaginary, thinking?"

Once we established that God can be only who He is and not who we imagine Him to be, we turned our discussion to the Bible. Is it God's Word? How can it be? And what does it say?

God gave me a great gift as we continued to talk. He gave me the boldness to address the issue of the stones and rational explanations of who He is. He gave me clarity to present a biblical gospel message.

Jonathan knew he wasn't perfect and acknowledged that he was doing things he shouldn't be doing. But he did not know that it was wrong to put stock in the stones.

We were standing in the middle of the infield at a NASCAR racetrack as crew members were preparing race trucks for competition. In essence, I presented the following plan of salvation:

- All have sinned and fall short of the glory of God. God loves us, but He is also holy.
- The wages of sin is death. That means that we're separated from God when we die.
- While we were yet sinners, Christ died for us.

As I shared John 3:16, Jonathan started to break. I asked him if he wanted to make a decision, a commitment to the Lord Jesus Christ. He was ready to come to Jesus.

While we headed to the lounge in our hauler, I asked him about the stones. We left them at the back of the hauler. He told me he had a bag of stones back at his house, and his kids slept with them under their pillows.

In the hauler we reviewed God's plan, His Word, His love,

and why Jesus had to die. Things got really quiet. Then through prayer Jonathan made the best decision he had ever made—he chose Jesus as his Lord and Savior. He got up with a bounce and a spring in his step. When we got to the back of the trailer, I asked, "What about the stones?" At his request, I gathered them up and threw them into the trashcan.

Jerry Punch, an ESPN commentator, came by to check on my medical status. He's a Christian, so I shared with him what the Lord had done at Atlanta and again this morning. He rejoiced with me. I was really getting excited.

Later the General Motors program manager stopped by for a visit. I shared with him what neat things happen when the gospel is presented.

Steve Portengaus of Bakersfield, California, was our driver for the weekend. Steve knew the trucks, the track, and the competition and had raced in the truck series a few years earlier. We practiced fast.

As the race trucks where brought to the inspection line for qualifying, I noticed that one fan was particularly interested in our truck. He walked around it, studied it, and then started asking me some questions about one of our sponsors. Decals advertising *Left Behind*, the popular book series written by Jerry Jenkins and Tim Lahaye, were on our truck. Tyndale Publishing House had agreed to come on as one of our sponsors for the Miami race two weeks earlier, and we hadn't yet removed the decals from the truck.

The fan asked the question, "What does 'left behind' mean anyway?" He was actually an intern for the local television station and was at the track to cover Friday's event.

I answered, "'Left behind' means dying without Christ—you're left behind." Through God's love the two of us yielded to the working of the Holy Spirit, and right there in the middle of the race track, standing between two tractor trailers with support series cars running laps, this man made life's greatest decision. By the end of the day at the racetrack, I had also taken the opportunity to share Jesus with our driver and his fiancé.

When our team left the track it was getting late, and we were all hungry and tired. I started eating my dinner but was overcome with severe cramping. My neck could hardly support my head.

When I returned to my hotel room, all activities of the day started to come back. I was in pain, but I could not escape the reality of God's working through me this day. People had made decisions for the Lord—in fact, three in less than seven days. Wow! I wanted to praise God for what was happening in my life. I opened the Gideon-placed Bible and started searching the Psalms. I looked earnestly for scripture that would express my heart for my Lord and Savior. The pain was gone. My heart was pounding, my eyes pouring, and I was speechless. Words could not express what I wanted to say to my Heavenly Father.

I read Ps. 71 as it led me to give praise to the Lord. As I read verse 24, I thought, *If only my tongue could talk of God's righteousness all day long. If only every day I could be a witness for the Lord. If only I could be used in this way to give testimony of God's grace, His love, and His plan for us to come to Him. What a great joy to know that He has used me!*

After years and years as a Christian, sitting in church service after church service, trying to live the Christian life, chasing my dreams wide open, the light came on. God is God. He created us. He loves us. But He is holy. Only a repentant heart with faith in Jesus Christ can qualify us for heaven. And when I'm praying for lost souls, prepared to give the gospel, God has allowed me to participate in the most important work of all. I still can't say I know everything about God's will for my life. But one thing I do know for sure—it's God's will that no one should perish, and I get to share that great news.

Therefore, when I'm yielded to the Holy Spirit and with humility sharing Jesus with others, I know that I'm exactly where God wants me to be, doing exactly what He wants me to do. I'm in the center of His will! There's no better place to be.

Lord, make us the best winners of all: Kingdom workers—soul winners! No win on the track compares to the victory of leading someone to Jesus Christ. That is indeed what it means to win the ultimate race!

Randy MacDonald's *dream was to become a NASCAR racecar driver. He holds an honors degree in mechanical engineering from the University of Waterloo. In 25 years of racing, Randy has enjoyed the privilege of winning races and earning titles. He is president of MacDonald Motorsports, and his team competes in NASCAR Craftsman truck series races. He and his wife, Gina, have two daughters and live in High Point, North Carolina.*

Brent Williams
A Christian Cop?

"A Christian cop," my dad repeated, looking as if the concept completely escaped him. He stood there looking at me and then reluctantly agreed that there was a need for Christian police officers.

My parents and I had been debating my desire to be a police officer since my senior year in high school. Now I was preparing to leave for my senior year of college, and they were still trying to talk me out of it. They had optimistically suggested almost every other job title they could think of as an alternative—computer programmer, youth minister, salesman, construction foreman. They were constantly coming up with fresh ideas to sway me.

It was the topic of conversation between Dad and me at the family dinner table just a couple of days before I was to leave. He asked, "Don't you know that no one likes cops?" I agreed. But then I countered by asking him if he thought there was a *need* for Christian cops. I realized that if I could get him to agree there was a need, he would have to concede my point that I should be one. And he did—reluctantly.

Some people never find an occupation they feel they really belong in. That wasn't a problem for me. God had prepared me for this occupation early on, and I always felt a peace about becoming a policeman. I knew it was God's will for me, and that's why I never yielded to my parents' insistence that I look in other directions for my life's work.

Though I was sure of God's will when I became a policeman,

I often found myself in need of His grace and healing touch because of the things I witnessed or participated in when I was on the job. There's more to police work than car chases, gun battles, and rescuing children from near-death calamities. In 19 years I have seen some of that, but those sorts of challenges have not had the deepest impact on me.

Once I was called into a home with a Family Services worker and Juvenile Services detective to remove two young children, ages two and five, from their home. It would have been much easier if I had been rescuing these two children from abusive parents or drug-addicted parents—but that was not the case. In this home the mother was suffering from a mental condition and had fallen into a deep depression, so deep that she just sat in a chair and stared.

Family Services had been notified by a family member, and when the worker went to check on the children's welfare, the mother was in such a bad way that she could hardly answer the simplest of questions. The social worker and the detective who accompanied her decided that the mother was not able to care for her children. Consequently, they were ordered removed from the home until the mother could receive treatment for her mental and emotional condition. I was given the thankless task of going there and taking the children.

Of course, the kids didn't understand any of this. All they knew was that strangers were taking them away. As the social worker and the detective began explaining to the parents what was happening and what they needed to do to get their children back, the mother began to weep. The father tried to comfort her, but he was so grief-stricken that he had to sit down and bury his face in his hands.

As I walked from the house with the five-year-old girl in my arms, the child was crying for her mommy and reaching back over my shoulder with both arms. I thought my heart would break. I kept telling myself that I was doing the right thing, but it didn't feel like it. I knew the parents would get their children back when the mother had dealt with her problems, and I knew the children would be safer somewhere else for the time being, but seeing this family devastated and torn apart was one of the hardest things I've witnessed. I felt like a monster. I truly needed God's grace that day.

And He was faithful. Later that day I stopped in front of a small, neat house where the foster parents lived who had agreed to take care of the children. A cheerful lady in her mid-50s met me in the driveway with a big smile on her face and a doll in her hands. She went straight to the passenger's side of the patrol car, opened the door, and knelt down. She began talking to the little girl and asked her if she would be able to help care for the doll. The child agreed, and suddenly she was in the arms of the foster parent. My heartache began to subside as I realized that God had sent His grace and peace to me and these children. It wasn't a major crime case, but God had called me to move these children to a safe haven.

Recently I was called upon to inform a woman that her husband had died unexpectedly while preparing for work. I was able to console her and assist her with the removal of his body from their home. Next I counseled a father who was having problems with a teenaged daughter who had run away and then had to arrest a prostitute with an habitual drug habit. She was high at the time and very belligerent. Her four-year-old daughter was with her. All of this was in the span of just a few hours.

It's because of days like this that I thank God for His grace and mercy that always get me through. I'm thankful that He uses me.

God is true to His Word. Rom. 10:13 tells us, "Whosoever shall call upon the name of the Lord shall be saved" (KJV). That's me; I'm "whosoever."

I've been weak at times. I've stumbled, and I've fallen. But I've never despaired. God is with me, and I know He wants me to succeed. Furthermore, He will help me succeed. James 1:4-5 says, "Let patience have her perfect work, that ye may be perfect and entire, wanting nothing. If any of you lack wisdom, let him ask of God, that giveth to all men liberally, and unbraideth not; and it shall be given him" (KJV). I have prayed for wisdom many, many times. And each time God has shown me the way. It may not have been the way I was expecting, but He has answered me nonetheless.

I love my job, and I'm certain it's my calling. God ministers to me daily, and that's what allows me to continue my work as "a Christian cop." I find joy in knowing that I'm making a difference in my world and that I'm pleasing my Heavenly Father. And just for the record—my earthly father is pleased too.

Brent Williams *is a veteran police officer in Overland Park, Kansas, and is a graduate of MidAmerica Nazarene University. He is the recipient of numerous service awards. He and his wife, Teresa, live with their two children in Overland Park.*

Ron Mehl

UNDER THE WATCHFUL EYE OF GOD

My grandmother always used to tell me, "Remember now, Ronnie—the eye of God is watching you everywhere you go, night and day." Somehow it wasn't much of a comfort when she said it—and I'm not sure it was meant to be. All I could picture was a large, roving, bloodshot eye floating behind me, tracking every move.

But God is more than an eye—He's a Person. He's a wise Father who loves us, concerns himself with us, and is acquainted with all our ways. His kind regard and constant attention ought to fill our hearts with courage.

It's easier to stand up to the neighborhood bully when you know your daddy is watching you from the front window.

It's easier to knock on your neighbor's door to apologize for breaking a window if your mom is standing a discreet distance behind you.

It's easier for an ambassador to draw a line in the sand in front of a puffed-up dictator when American F-16s are cruising the sky.

It's easier to face life with boldness and confidence when you realize the God of the universe watches every step you take, every move you make. With that knowledge in your heart, you'll attempt things and step into situations you otherwise would not!

I've always wondered why Peter seemed so bold and fearless at times. As I've pondered that thought, it has come to me that

Peter was brave when he knew the Lord was standing nearby—watching him.

He could climb over the side of a boat in the middle of a black night onto a stormy sea and walk on the whitecaps—because Jesus was standing on the water, too, just a few yards away.

He could pull out his sword in front of an angry mob and lop off the ear of the high priest's servant—because he knew Jesus was right behind him.

Yes, his courage failed in the courtyard of Caiaphas when a servant girl's words led him to deny he even knew Jesus. Peter did not know that the Lord was near enough to see, but He was. Scripture tells us, "The Lord turned and looked at Peter," and the heartbroken disciple "went out and wept bitterly" (Luke 22:61-62, NKJV)

After the Resurrection, Peter was bolder than ever. He preached to a crowd of thousands, charged his fellow Jews with crucifying the Messiah, and coolly informed the assembled Jewish leadership that he was answerable to God rather than them. Their response to his fire and courage is worth noting.

"Now when they saw the boldness of Peter and John, and perceived that they were uneducated and untrained men, they marveled. And they realized that they had been with Jesus" (Acts 4:13, NKJV).

Peter and John not only had been with Jesus—they still were! They were filled with the Holy Spirit, and the promise of their beloved Lord still rang in their ears: "Lo, I am with you always, even to the end of the age" (Matt. 28:20, NKJV).

Whether we fully understand and appreciate it or not, He's with us in the same way. How we need to cultivate that sense of His presence!

I was grateful that I had cultivated His presence before the day I walked into my doctor's office. After what I thought was a routine physical, my family doctor called me into his office and said, "Ron, the news is not good. You have leukemia—a slow-moving form of cancer."

He didn't have to explain. A pastor friend of mine in Minneapolis had just died of that disease. I knew about leukemia; I just couldn't believe that *I* had it. It was as if someone had grabbed my life's book out of my hands, flipped through the pages, and then handed it back to me.

I found myself staring at the last chapter—long before I ever wanted or expected to. Receiving that kind of news is like a punch in the stomach. It knocks the wind out of us. So many thoughts flashed through my mind: *Where do I turn? Who do I tell? What should I say? What shouldn't I say?* So many questions—so much confusion. Yet the Jesus who had stood by Peter and John was standing there with me. I would be able to—by His grace and strength—face an uncertain future. Like Peter, I would step out of my boat and walk on top of this stormy sea.

You see, my grandmother was right. The eye of God *is* watching me. Moreover, the presence of God is giving me the strength I need. I will walk on top of my storm, and because He is still here with me in my world today, I will find joy in the road upon which He has placed me—even though it takes me into some uncomfortable territory.

The eye of God is indeed watching me.

Ron Mehl made his final journey May 30, 2003. His joy is now complete.

Ron Mehl *was a pastor, loving husband, devoted father, and best-selling author. His books include Gold Medallion winners* **God Works the Night Shift** *and* **The Tender Commandments.** *He lived with his wife, Joyce, in Beaverton, Oregon.*

Graeme Lee

FAITH IN A HOSTILE ENVIRONMENT

I vividly remember the gray, forbidding day in November 1981 when I walked through the doors of Parliament in Wellington, New Zealand, for the first time.

It was a day of mixed emotions. I was elated to be finally entering the "prison house," but I was apprehensive about my ability to do what was required of me in that tense cauldron. And the cauldron had just gotten hotter. Parliament now had a one-seat majority, commonly referred to as a "hung parliament." With Robert Muldoon reelected as prime minister, the shock waves were about to begin.

I wasn't fearful, because I knew this was the place of God's appointment for me. But one thing was clear—this was going to be a hostile environment.

My definition of a hostile environment is a place where Christian behavior is barely tolerated and Christian outspokenness is opposed. In my case, the Parliament of New Zealand is regarded as a hostile environment. Your environment could be a workplace where most or all of your colleagues don't believe in Christianity. Perhaps your manager or superior sets the tone and imposes his or her anti-Christian views in a belligerent manner, making it very difficult to talk about your faith.

Maybe it's a home where spouses are divided—one is a believer and the other is not. Possibly a member of the family has become a Christian, and the parents and other siblings are not. It could be a health challenge or even a major terrible tragedy.

A hostile environment is any circumstance in which sharing

and living out your faith is tough. If that's so for you, be encouraged. God knows everything, and He's going to help you grow and use you in a way that you could not believe. Your part is to trust Him.

However, what's happening for many believers is quite the opposite: opposition leads to tension, and tension leads to depression; depression leads to serious doubts about whether it's all worthwhile.

It's easy to say, "It shouldn't be so." It's another thing to be in such a position and maintain your faith.

How can you do this? I don't purport to have all the answers, but I do know what God has done for me. In fact, I want to tell you that God will walk beside you through your struggles and will not only help you to maintain your faith but also strengthen it.

How important is this issue? Very. It's my observation that many of God's people are having real struggles at school, work, or in their families.

People read about victorious Christian living and want to live like that seven days a week, but somehow it doesn't happen. So excuses are made, such as "If you knew what I had to put up with, you would understand."

True disciples don't look for excuses. I well remember having the privilege of speaking in Russia at the Moscow Baptist Church in 1974. I shared the simple message that we in the free world had not forgotten them and that we loved them and covenanted to pray for them. Lauris and I were deeply moved to see the tears that flowed all around that auditorium as they received those words through the interpreter. As we hurriedly left before the end of the service to catch a flight to London, people came into the aisles to hug and embrace us. Our interpreter accompanied us to the nearest taxi, and we learned firsthand from her about truly living victoriously in a hostile environment.

As a child she had watched her father and mother killed for their faith. She described the living conditions for a confessed Christian in Russia—conditions we in the free world could not even begin to understand. But we did not hear a word of complaint, bitterness, or self-pity from her—just thankfulness at the goodness of God in her life. What real faith!

The following are seven guidelines for living a powerful life of faith.

First: Get going. Don't slump back into indecision, as the children of Israel did when they were confronted by the Red Sea. You're in the right place—just get going. In Parliament whenever the going got tough, I would say to myself, *This is God's appointed place for me.* That automatically makes every day an adventure. Even if I knew about a looming showdown with the press or a tough speech in a crisis, I still looked forward to the start of every day. To me, faith is in every sense of the word an adventure with God.

Second: Be consistent. Your life can speak louder than words. People want to see a life that's consistent with your profession of being a new creation in Christ. They don't look for perfection, but they do observe how you react to the challenges of life and particularly your attitude toward others.

Third: Be real. Don't try to be like everybody else and try to make everybody like you. That might be the way you succeed in politics, but it lasts only for a season. Jesus was a realist and was honest about the consequences of following Him. He said that if you follow Him, many people would not approve of your decision. That's certainly true in the world of politics.

As the world gets more and more secular, it's also becoming more and more hostile toward Christianity. We need to be real. The Bible says that everyone who wants to live a godly life in Christ Jesus will be persecuted. This does not mean that we go around looking for persecution or hide away but rather seek good relationships with all people with the knowledge of God's teaching.

Fourth: Expect adversity. Recognize the source of adversity, and don't retaliate. Refusing to retaliate is certainly anathema in politics. But if you really think about it, you'll realize that this is where the whole world has gone wrong. The devil is the enemy of God, but because he cannot get at God, he does the next best thing—he tries to hurt God's children. So recognize the source. Remember this great principle of life: You have control of your reaction. You don't have to retaliate. Your faith will grow as a result.

Fifth: Be a "can do" person. Be positive, and always maintain a happy disposition. You can't have a victorious faith if you're negative and morose. I've observed several professing Christians in Parliament over a period of time who have substantially lost their faith and lost their way. They have become quite negative and critical. When you allow yourself to get on the negative treadmill, the spiral seems always to go down and down.

Expect to grow and not groan. I say as a public testimony to God that my faith was stronger when I left Parliament than when I entered it 15 years earlier. I'm not bragging—far from it. I believe we should be growing in God wherever we are. Others will take notice, especially if we're in the same place they are but visibly find strength outside ourselves whereas they flounder.

Sixth: Share your faith. Serving Christ and sharing our faith is the greatest privilege we have. In spite of this, we often tend to live our lives building our own kingdoms rather than helping to build God's kingdom. Our purpose above everything else should be to please our Lord. That's where real faith comes into action. Heb. 11:6 reminds us that without faith it is impossible to please God, because anyone who comes to Him must believe that He exists and that He rewards those who earnestly seek Him.

Seventh: Rejoice in the Lord. We have every reason to rejoice. The Bible tells us that we should praise God at all times, which means that we should be joyful at all times. We can't praise God without being joyful. So it doesn't matter how difficult your circumstances or how dire the situation. We should be seen as joyful overcomers.

We should also recognize that we're strengthened in our joy. The Bible says that the joy of the Lord is our strength (Neh. 8:10). So as we express joy as overcomers and resist sinking back into our own struggles, we're actually made stronger.

Joy is very important in facing a hostile environment. We can get going, be consistent, maintain a positive attitude, and witness—but still not fully succeed. Joy is the one ingredient that makes all these things come together and allows us to be victorious and full of faith for every moment of life.

Graeme Lee *came to prominence as a mayor in New Zealand and went on to serve as a member of Parliament for 15 years. During that time he became the Minister of Internal Affairs and was the founder of the Christian Democratic Party. He and his wife, Lauris, have three married daughters and live in Auckland, New Zealand.*

Ray Cook
FAITH TO GIVE

I was raised in a pastor's home, and I heard early and often about faith. My dad did more than just preach about faith in God and His Word—he lived it. And there were times when faith in God was all we had. So I learned at a young age to live a life of absolute trust in God. It's that attitude that has fueled my desire to give to others.

I've been extremely blessed. My medical practice has prospered, and business enterprises I've been a part of have done very well. One of my former pastors once told me, "I believe God is looking for some people He can afford to prosper. He wants to bless people he can trust to channel financial resource to points of need." I've been blessed to be one of those individuals.

I love to give. In fact, I would rather give than get. Not that I don't like gifts myself, but life has taught me to redefine what I consider a gift—for instance, the look on my wife's face, sometimes with tears, when I bring home a special surprise, like flowers. The gift I'm giving then becomes all mine.

Perhaps there have been times in your life when you've given a gift but you ended up being the recipient of the greater gift because you were blessed by the happiness you caused.

About five years ago I asked that my children and their families change the way they give me gifts. I asked them to spend the intended gift money on a needy family or child. That would be my gift—and theirs. Now one of the highlights of our gift-opening sessions is to hear what was done and how it was received. Yes, someone else received a gift, but I believe I receive an even greater one.

At times I give anonymously, and that's really fun. At other times the recipient of my gift didn't respond the way I expected, and I've had to find joy in just knowing that what I did was indeed needed.

On some occasions when I've given a gift, my motive was misinterpreted. A few years ago I gave the wife of each of our pastors enough money to buy themselves a new Christmas outfit. Six of the ladies were surprised and thrilled. But one of them seemed a little hurt and asked, "Do I look like I really need a new outfit?"

The Bible is explicit about being generous. Prov. 25 tells us to be generous to our enemies and surprise them with goodness. Prov. 28 exhorts us to be generous to the poor.

Over the years I've given watches to many friends. I always ask that they not mention the giver, and then I just stand back and watch them enjoy their gifts. I'm twice blessed—once for them and once for me.

Clothes, shoes, money, smiles—so much to give away and so little time! I've never been able to give away more than God has given me. In fact, the only things in life that I've kept are the things I gave away.

It was a great blessing to be raised in a pastor's home and learn the lessons of faith in God—faith for salvation, yes, but beyond that, faith that God provides for the needs of His people. That faith has freed me to give generously to others and to experience the great joy of being used by God.

Ray Cook, M. D., has practiced family care medicine for 30 years. He is a successful businessman who has used his resources in strong support of his church on all levels. He and his wife, Elaine, have two adult children and live in Wichita, Kansas.

Tex Reardon
GOD IS AT WORK IN OUR LIVES

I accepted Christ at a youth fellowship meeting over the Christmas holidays during my sophomore year of high school. The pastor of the small Methodist church in Ventnor, New Jersey, that I attended encouraged young people to take part in church activities. He encouraged us to be ushers and sing in the choir, and thus the church had a great youth group during a time in our society when young people, especially teenagers, were to be seen and not heard.

I dropped away from church when I went away to college. The pastors of the churches I visited seemed to be preaching from the front page of the newspaper rather than from the Bible.

I married during my junior year of college in 1952 but remained disenchanted with church attendance. In 1965 we moved to West Palm Beach, Florida. Up to that time I had considered myself a good Christian and felt that I didn't need to go to church. When we arrived in West Palm Beach, however, God began to escalate His influence in my life. My mother-in-law urged me to attend her church, and I eventually agreed. The first Sunday morning I attended, the pastor, Jess Moody, preached from James 1:22—"Be ye doers of the word, and not hearers only, deceiving your own selves" (KJV). I felt that he was preaching straight to me alone, and I recommitted my life to Christ and was privileged to be baptized with my three sons.

I subsequently became very active in the church and in evangelism. I was part of the first group in our church to go through the Evangelism Explosion program and became an instructor. When Dr. Moody left the church and a new pastor was being called, I served as Sunday School superintendent. We called Betty Fisher to come and work with our Sunday School adult program. She became a great friend and associate.

Betty began encouraging me to go into full-time Christian service. I kept reminding her that I was deeply involved in starting a new business and that I was not cut out for full-time service.

Betty and her husband, Lee, went to a Billy Graham team meeting, and when she returned she became even more persistent in urging me into full-time Christian work. Her favorite line was "The Lord is telling me you need to be in His service." I finally asked her why the Lord was talking to her and not me, and her answer was, "You're not listening, and He needs someone to get your attention."

One afternoon she came into my office and said that the Billy Graham team had a need and that she wouldn't leave until I talked with Sterling Huston. We called Sterling, but I told him I was not interested because I was heavily involved in starting a new business. He asked if I would send a résumé and my personal testimony, and I agreed to do that.

Three months later, I faced the fact that my business venture was too big and demanded too much money. A banker friend urged me to close it down and pay off all the debts. In his opinion, I would then be broke but at least would not have to declare bankruptcy. I decided to take his advice. On the last day we were in our house, God called in the person of Sterling Huston of the Billy Graham Evangelistic Association. He was checking to see if anything had changed with me and if I would be interested in interviewing for a job opening in their organization. I made arrangements to travel to Minneapolis to meet with him and was there offered the opportunity to join the Billy Graham

Evangelistic Association. I accepted, and so in 1977 I was assigned to the crusade team in Kansas City.

Thus began a long and fulfilling career with the Billy Graham team. In March 1998 my wife of 45 years passed away very suddenly. I was left with a house in Houston plus my 89-year-old mother and 89-year-old mother-in-law to care for. My mother-in-law passed away five months after my wife died, and it became necessary for my mother to go into an assisted living facility in Austin, Texas, near my oldest son and his family. I moved back to Minneapolis and began work on the Amsterdam Conference.

This conference was a tremendous training conference for more than 11,000 itinerant evangelists from more than 200 countries and territories around the world. It also held special meaning for me since I met my second wife as a result of that conference. I had been sure I would never remarry, but God brought Sandy into my life, blessing me with a second mate who loved Him as much as I did and was a perfect complement to me and the ministry to which God had called me. We were married shortly after the conclusion of the Amsterdam 2000 conference.

I was then asked by Franklin Graham to direct "Prescription for Hope," an international conference sponsored by Samaritan's Purse to encourage the church to be more involved in the HIV/AIDS pandemic. This pandemic has afforded one of the greatest evangelistic opportunities the Church has seen. For those not infected with this deadly virus, a personal relationship with Jesus and adherence to God's instruction for fidelity in marriage and abstinence before marriage are the only sure way to remain uninfected. For those who are already infected, their hope is in eternity and the promise that comes through a personal relationship with Jesus. It has given the Church the opportunity to become less judgmental and to take a more proactive position in the care and witness to the millions affected by this devastating disease.

I look back over my life and see how God prepared me for the challenges and opportunities He has put before me. My association with the Billy Graham Evangelistic Association has given me an outlet for my passion for evangelism and for constantly seeking new and better ways to reach more people with the good news of the gospel. God promises never to ask us to do anything He has not prepared us for.

Tex Reardon *is manager of the Billy Graham Evangelistic Association transition office in Charlotte, North Carolina. He has been a vital part of that organization since 1977. He is the father of four children. He and his wife, Sandy, live in Ft. Mill, South Carolina.*

Stan Boggs
GOD ALWAYS HAS A PLAN

I was eager to get to work following my graduation from Southwest College in Winfield, Kansas. I learned of a teaching and coaching position in Cimarron, Kansas, a small western Kansas town of 1,800. After going to Cimarron for an interview, I was offered the position, and my wife, Pat, and I discussed moving there. We felt it would be good for us to venture out on our own, and Cimarron seemed like a good place to start. We were right. What we didn't know at the time was that the little town we planned to call home for the first few years of our marriage would be home for 25 years.

I had faith in God in those days and considered myself a Christian. I didn't attend church, but I believed in God and did my best to live a good life.

I felt something was missing in my life and didn't have much peace. Even though I enjoyed my teaching and coaching career and Pat enjoyed her job and we had a wonderful baby girl, something just didn't feel quite complete.

Cimarron has five Protestant churches in town, and a Catholic church is just six miles down the road. We knew the pastors of all the churches and members of each congregation. We visited four of the churches and enjoyed each one but still couldn't decide which to attend.

To complete our round, we visited the fifth Protestant church in Cimarron. The moment we entered the church, we knew we were home. We knew we were where God wanted us and I was certain that this body of believers could help me find that something that was missing from my life.

Finally we were part of a church family. We continued to seek advice and wisdom from our families back in Winfield, but we loved our new church friends and the new dimension they brought to our lives. We shared belief in God. We enjoyed being together, and we enjoyed raising our kids together, helping each other out with projects around our homes and at church and even taking vacations together. The church family stood together through good times and bad times.

The men and boys in our church often enjoyed camping trips together. On one of those trips, to Table Rock Lake in Missouri, the adults sat around the campfire one evening talking about the importance of baptism. Several of us asked the pastor if he would baptize us, and the next evening we held a baptism service in Table Rock Lake. What a beautiful sight—men and boys of all ages serving public notice that they loved Jesus!

Not everything in the church family went smoothly all the time, of course. There were disagreements and sometimes hurt feelings. Occasionally we lost much-loved members to other congregations. But it's OK to disagree, and we respected each other's decisions.

After we had enjoyed around 25 years in our little town, a cousin of mine passed through and asked me if I ever planned to move from there. I really hadn't given it much thought. We had lived there a long time, and I enjoyed my position with the school, and Pat enjoyed her job. We had raised our family there, and our house would be paid for in three short years. Why would we leave?

Not long after that conversation with my cousin I was reading the Bible when I came across this passage in 1 Tim. 5:8—"If anyone does not provide for his own, and especially for those of his household, he has denied the faith and is worse than an unbeliever" (NKJV). That verse grabbed me.

Pat's parents and mine were doing well. Still, we were more than 200 miles away from them, and there would likely come the day when they needed our help. We prayed about this and held family discussions about it.

I asked Pat to read the scripture, and she asked, "Do you think we should move closer to home?"

After much prayer and discussion, I applied for a job in Winfield—the town that held so many wonderful memories from college days. I was offered a position in the school system, and I accepted.

It's amazing how God worked out the details of selling our house and buying a home in Winfield. When moving day arrived, our Cimarron church family showed up, some using a vacation day from work, and we loaded up and formed a caravan to Winfield, 250 miles away.

When we arrived in Winfield on that humid summer day, we were greeted by 20 hot, tired members of our new Christian family who were awaiting our arrival. They didn't know us personally, but that didn't stop them from coming to help. They had just moved another member of the church into a new house that same day, so they were doing double duty. Thus began a new phase in our lives.

Not everything went smoothly. It took Pat a while to find a job; there were cutbacks in the state education budgets, and I came close to losing my new job, and our son went away to college and left Pat and me alone in our new empty nest.

We faced some difficulties when my father underwent several surgeries and our first grandchild was born with a condition that required hospitalization. But because God's plan for us was playing out, we were right where we needed to be. Praise God for the confidence in knowing that He's directing our paths!

It's true—you can believe in God without attending church. But with whom do you worship? With whom do you pray? Who shares your concerns, your fears, your burdens, your joys? The day I quit wrestling with God about my "independence" was the beginning of a life of joy. His plan for me has been greater than anything I might have designed, and my family and I have the peace of knowing we're right where He wants us to be.

Stan Boggs *has been a high school teacher and coach for many years. He and his wife, Pat, have been married nearly 30 years. They have two children and one grandson. Stan teaches Sunday School and is part of his church's worship team. The Boggs family lives in Winfield, Kansas.*

Todd Tiahrt

GOVERNING BY FAITH

The chairperson slams the gavel. Stomach muscles tighten, and hands fidget. A heavy tension makes the air difficult to breathe. Once again, silence sweeps the room. The debate is over.

Surrounded by a sea of faces, two members of Congress stand in a deafening stillness, eyes staring. The dark red carpet is lost beneath the chairs, tables, and polished shoes. Behind the chairperson deep maroon drapes and dark wood paneling extend the length of the wall. The room is hot. Ears perk, heads turn, and cameras pan toward the committee chairperson.

Some issues are shirked at the grocery store, the beauty parlor, or even our churches because they're too intense. But in the capital city of the United States, they boil in a near volcanic way. Evaluating the value of human life, handing out needles to drug abusers, using foreign aid to pay for abortions—these issues are fueled by emotion. Yet these topics are constantly being debated, and the outcomes determine how we're going to govern ourselves on a national level. Ideas eventually become the world in which our children live. Therefore, addressing these matters must be faced without trepidation. Faith must temper how we decide what side we choose, what outcome we support, and what choices we make.

The chairperson recognizes me.

I remain standing. Without speaking, I gather my thoughts. What can I say about the value of human life that will effectively reflect the essence of my faith? What can I draw from the depths of my soul to communicate the urgent need for our culture to acknowledge God's greatest gift, the gift of life? Where is my strength? Where are the words? I try to ignore the cameras. I contemplate longer. My words seem so inadequate to express what my heart so deeply feels. What will paint a picture each person will remember? I must do my best to represent my God-given beliefs.

The members of Congress can be divided into two broad categories. On one side you have members who believe solutions to problems can be found through the creation of government programs, a faith in the ability of government to answer almost every problem. On the other side, you have members who believe less government and more personal responsibility are the keys to answering some of our most difficult problems.

The founding fathers of the United States understood these two competing philosophies and the dangers associated with shirking personal responsibility. They set in motion a government they believed reflected universal laws as given by Almighty God. They established a government in which *individual responsibility* was paramount to a healthy, vibrant society.

We're now in the first few years of the 21st century, and residents of the United States are still battling the notion that government can provide answers for all our troubles. I'm thankful our founders had the wisdom to lay scriptural principles as the bedrock of our federal government.

As individuals in the kingdom of God, we also have personal responsibility. We can either accept or reject God's plan. God has allowed us to freely love or hate, and He does not force either upon us. We alone are responsible for the decision to accept the Lord's redemptive grace. God, in infinite wisdom, has designed the world in that fashion, giving us opportunity to do right.

The United States acknowledges certain inalienable rights. Among those rights are life, liberty, and the pursuit of happiness. The founding fathers wanted to limit the federal government from intruding upon these rights so each person would be free and enjoy liberty, which I define as the freedom to do the right thing. Just as God trusts us individually with His love, so we believe the government should not interfere with individual responsibility and freedom unless that trust has been broken.

A society will disintegrate from within when its government steals from the people their motivation for acting as responsible citizens. For those whose faith continues to reside in the government, problems will only continue to mushroom. The people, their hope now in government, have lost the will to act in the responsibility of freedom.

Their view says that if we have crime, it's because there are not enough jobs for people. If we have hunger, it's because we don't have a program to distribute food. If we have child abuse or abandoned children, it's because poor women don't have access to abortion through all nine months of pregnancy, funded by a government program. If the world's population is growing too fast, it's because we're not using our foreign aid dollars to promote sterilization, contraceptives, or abortion. If we have a problem, we're only one government program away from a solution. At best there is but a faded memory of a time when people were able to take care of themselves. Now only the government can solve the problems facing us. We're just victims of a system that's under-funded and too small.

This philosophy was once verbalized by a previous president when he said, "Sure, we could give you a tax break—but then we would have to trust you to spend it properly."

In that one sentence is captured the philosophy of those whose trust is in government. They've told us that our money is not really ours—it belongs to the government. We're not to be trusted to make our own decisions, because government knows better how to take care of us than we do ourselves.

We want good jobs. We want housing. We want healthcare. We want retirement. We want free schooling. We want all that makes us happy and content. But in the end, the job is not really the job we want. The house is in a dangerous neighborhood. The healthcare plan is too restrictive. The retirement payments are not adequate for meeting the bills. And our children are graduating without being able to read. Maybe we need more funding. One only wonders how our founding fathers would have viewed this philosophy.

The United States has checks and balances in the legislative, executive, and judicial branches of our government. Each legislative body, the Senate and the House of Representatives, has majority and minority parties. It seems to be designed so that no one person, no one political party, or even one branch of government is too strong, too intrusive. In this nation's design, not even the president can demand his or her own way. It is by wise foresight that we have a system of liberty in which individuals are able to determine their own destiny without government intrusion.

As I begin to speak, my chest tightens with emotion and I feel the glares intensifying. The lights, smirks, cameras, and creased foreheads all seem to be aimed at me. You can smell the discomfort, even rage. It is like a fog. My words are simple and straightforward. Members shift in their chairs, some quietly cheering for me. Others lean forward, hands clenched and jaws locked. I am not known as an eloquent speaker, but my thoughts are clear. And I never back down from a fight when standing for what I believe is right.

I smile. Once again life comes back into focus, and the haze seems to have vanished. This may be another tough battle over the soul of our nation, but I know I am not alone. I am just one man standing shoulder to shoulder with many other believers. Every day someone is holding me up in prayer. Every day the

Holy Spirit lays upon the heart of another believer to stand with me in this battle. Today I am on the front line, facing down the enemy. But I stand with a great company of supporters. Joy swells in my soul.

I am reminded that human life is a gift from God, and we are called to protect it, despite being part of a society where convenience is made a god. What is communicated in our pop culture is that a pregnant woman does not become a mother until she wants the child, until the child is convenient for her lifestyle. For some Americans, unborn children are only tissue and do not qualify for basic human rights.

As a freshman in Congress, I sat on the Science Committee and listened to a scientist explain the need to protect endangered species. His example was a water turtle. Part of his testimony included when we should start the process of protection and for how long we should extend that safety. He stated that we should protect the turtle from the moment the egg was fertilized. I found the idea remarkable. If scientists know when life begins for endangered species, why not for the *human* species?

As Mother Teresa said at the National Prayer Breakfast in 1994, "The greatest destroyer of peace today is abortion, because it is a war against the child."

She went on to say that both the mother and the father try to remove themselves from their personal responsibility to that child by destroying the child. What a tragedy!

The message of convenience is wrong for our young who need to grow up in a world that teaches them to treat others as they would like to be treated, to sacrifice, and to take ownership for their own actions. Violence in the womb only begets more problems.

I summarize before the committee what I believe to be right. The debate ends. I sit back into my chair. My hands are warm, and I can feel the nerve pulses twitching in my stomach. I thank

God that my voice was clear and steady instead of clattering like a can dragging behind a car. Minutes will have to pass before I feel totally at rest. The adrenaline subsides, and I am at peace. I have fought the good fight today. Joy is alive in my heart.

The joy of the Lord is our strength (Neh. 8:10). Our God grants us strength in times of need. He gave Moses strength when he confronted Pharaoh. David spoke in the Psalms of God's strength. Jesus received it the night before His crucifixion in the Garden of Gethsemane. And with the strength from God in the midst of our weakness comes joy. The joy of the Lord gives us strength, and that in turn gives us joy. Joy follows in the knowledge that we're not in this fight alone—that our Creator will meet our most urgent needs.

Sometimes we forget that we're in a battle for the soul of our nation. It's fought every day in our homes, our churches, our schools, our communities, our state or provincial capitals, and in our nation's capital. Sooner or later, all of us will receive a call to pick up the standard and defend our faith. In doing so, let us go forward in the joy of the Lord.

One of the greatest joys of my life has come from being trusted by God and the people of my congressional district to do all I can to help our nation remain under the safekeeping of our Heavenly Father.

That is living by faith.

Todd Tiahrt *is a United States representative and has served the Fourth District of Kansas in Congress since 1995. He is a champion of traditional American values. He is a member of several high-profile committees and has received numerous honors. He and his wife, Vicki, live in Fairfax, Virginia. They have three children.*

Joe White
A Story of Grace

My Christian walk began when I was a 17-year-old student at the summer camp my parents founded in Branson, Missouri —Kamp Kanakuk. Kids come from all across North America to attend Kamp Kanakuk, a Christian youth camp that emphasizes sports.

Late one night as we sat under an oak tree, a camp counselor talked to me about accepting Christ as my personal Savior. I prayed the sinner's prayer and became a believer that night. I didn't feel the earth move or see fireworks or anything like that, but I did feel a sense of peace, and I knew that my sins were forgiven.

During the years that followed, my Christian walk was an unsteady one, and my Christian witness was not all that God wanted it to be.

I married while I was still in college, and our lives revolved around my last two seasons of college football. After graduation I got a job in a small town that required me to be out of town a great deal of the time. My wife and my good friend became attracted to one another, and suddenly my marriage ended.

I felt tremendous pain and guilt because of the failure of my marriage. But it was through this trying time that God reached down and revealed himself to me as my Father. His compassion felt like a father's arms wrapped around me in comfort and love. That's when I became completely His. From that point forward I knew who I was in Him and allowed Him to use my life for His glory.

I eventually recovered from the pain and began to realize that God would allow me to love again. I met a beautiful girl, Debbie Jo, and that summer God led her to become a counselor at our sports camp. Because God had instructed me to forgive my first wife and my friend, and His Spirit had helped me do that, I was free to give Debbie Jo all my love and never look back. We married, and together we now have four beautiful children.

I would like to say I entered a happily-ever-after existence, but that isn't the case. One summer my daughter Courtney attended one of our camps for 13 days. We ask parents not to visit until the closing ceremonies, and after a few days Courtney became homesick. Her counselor dried her tears and assured her that she was doing great, was growing spiritually, and would soon be back home.

"I never get to see my dad," Courtney protested. The counselor didn't know what to say. When the camp director heard the story, he made a beeline to my office. As he told me the story, I dug my chin deeper into my hands and wished I could melt into the chair. Instead of focusing on my kids, I had been absorbed in work.

The director wasn't easy on me. He said, "We're not leaving this room until you make some serious commitments. Joe, your life is going to change—and I'm going to hold you accountable to it."

The sad truth is that my oldest son learned to ride his bike with the help of his babysitter. My oldest daughter used to put notes on my desk asking for an appointment. I was a workaholic, and I left my wife and four children begging for my attention. But before I could give the attention, God had to get mine.

After that talk with the camp director, I began to invest my time in my wife and kids. By God's grace I became a husband and father.

By grace I got on the right track. I've begun to delegate jobs in the workplace, and I've learned to say no to long hours so that I can say yes to bedtime stories. Many nights I pray, *Lord make me a more effective dad.*

I have no trophies to display, but I have four growing children and a wife who is my best friend. My kids love their parents and their God.

I was feeling that my life was on track when my physician and friend, Buddy Rawlings, came to see me a couple of days after I went to have a blood profile done because of some unusual bruising on the back of my legs.

"Joe," he said, "I have some bad news for you. The blood tests indicate some problems I need to discuss with you. You have leukemia."

I was numb. How could I tell my wife? What about my kids? They were 25, 23, 22, and 18. I had dreamed about their weddings, prayed for their future spouses, and looked forward to becoming a grandparent.

Over the next few days the tears flowed in our family. And we turned to the Lord.

We were suddenly on a roller coaster. I heard about miracle cures and about the "normal" course of leukemia. I would pray in thanksgiving and then hold my wife as she wept. Friends who meant well sent me cures of fruit and vegetable pills, cures with carrots, cures with barley, cures with soy, cures with water filters, and news of cures in Mexico, Minnesota, and Oregon. I received hundreds of letters, E-mails, and phone calls.

I was hanging on the cross of a potentially fatal blood disease.

And then I saw a Man hanging on the cross beside me. His blood was pure enough to cleanse mine for eternity. He looked into the eyes of the thief hanging next to Him and then into my eyes. He saw my faith and spoke words of life into my deepest fears.

Today you will be with Me in paradise.

The grace of God once again flooded my heart, and I saw my life through His eyes. I've learned the secret of contentment in all situations. I have the heart knowledge that God is in control regardless of the situation. All He asks is that I let go and let Him have it.

God has given me an even greater passion for young people. I meet thousands of them at our camp, and I get to travel across the United States to speak to thousands more at colleges across the country. I love what I do and feel extremely blessed to do it. Young people are hungry to hear Christ's message and eager to accept it.

God has placed me a Kamp Kanakuk, where the focus is on Jesus and the joy He wants for every one of us. I'm in complete remission and am blessed to be His vessel to help these young people find joy in their lives. And that brings incredible joy into my life.

Joe White *is president of Kanakuk Youth Camps, located in Branson, Missouri. Each summer the camps host 20,000 college-age and professional staff. He is the author of 14 books and is in demand as a speaker for numerous events, including Promise Keepers and professional football and baseball chapels. He and his wife, Debbie, live in Branson. They have four adult children.*

Pat Williams
MOUNTAINTOP RESCUE

Has your life ever flashed before your eyes? You know—when a driver pulls out in front of you, you start to slide off a roof, your sister-in-law says, "I'll cook." In that split-second of terror you remember things you thought you had forgotten. Usually there's no time for reflection or sincere pondering. You avoid the car, you grab the gutter, your father-in-law says, "Hey—I have a coupon. Let's eat out." And just like that, you go on. I've had many of those experiences in my life. One Super Bowl Sunday, however—thanks to the Lord—I got to take a good look at my life: where I had been, who had been with me, and what I had done for 32 years.

I was raised in a preacher's home, so I understand completely the importance of being in church to worship our Lord on Sunday. Like many folks, though, I thought I could strike a bargain with God. At the time, I was enjoying my first year as the head football coach in a little town in western Wyoming, and one of my assistants invited me to go with him and some local townspeople to snowmobile.

What a great opportunity to witness! I told myself, although I would have to miss church in order to go with them. I figured this would give the guys the opportunity to discover that the new coach was a Christian. Bob, my assistant, had even promised to go to church with me the next Sunday. Why, I was practically saving people through snowmobiling! "Will we be back in time for kickoff?" was really my only question. This was, after all, Super Bowl Sunday. I was told it would be no problem to be in front of my television set by game time.

My first inkling that this was not going to be a normal day was when I asked where we would be riding.

"Devil's Hole," Bob said.

If you remember anything from this story, let it be this: Do not skip church to do *anything* in a place called "Devil's Hole."

After about an hour of snowmobiling, we reached Devil's Hole. The ride wasn't that bad. *OK—I was scared to death.* But there was no way I was going to show fear. I was grateful for that helmet and visor, though. We rode the machines down about a 300-foot drop at a 45- to 50-degree slope. Thankfully, the other guys couldn't tell the difference between screams of joy and screams of terror. I survived the drop into the hole, and we rode through canyons and timber for a couple of hours. Then I really started enjoying it.

The trouble started when I noticed it was about three o'clock, and I knew it would take a couple of hours to get back to the trucks and back to town. I had told my wife that I would be back around five. The other guys wanted to ride a bit longer. I told Bob that we should head back, because I would be the slowest rider and the others could catch up easily. Plus, I didn't want to miss kickoff. So Bob and I began making our way back.

To make a long story short, two and a half hours later, Bob and I were hopelessly lost. We had gotten stuck several times trying to ride out of a canyon we had mistakenly dropped in to, and we were physically exhausted. Now we were on a mountain, and every trail looped back to the top of it. We decided that since Bob was a better rider than me, he would quickly check several possible trails and come back for me when he found the right one. The sun was going down, and the wind was picking up. I had worked up a sweat digging our machines out after being stuck, and now my wet long-johns and socks added to my chill. I knew the temperature would drop to 10 or 15 degrees below zero that night, and as I sat there shivering, my life flashed before my eyes.

As a teenager I had spent years fighting religion. My daddy was a preacher, and I had gotten a good inside look at church politics: *I give the most, so I should control the budget. We don't feel So-and-so is qualified to teach this class, but we're too busy to help. If the music is that loud next Sunday, we're not coming back!* At the time I had confused all that with genuine Christianity, and I didn't want any part of it. I had turned to parties and friends who weren't "judgmental," and the worse I got, the cooler I thought I was.

Where did that lifestyle lead? To broken relationships, no true friends, and eventually a gun pointed at myself in a nearly successful suicide attempt.

I believe in angels. My mom died during my senior year in college. Knowing my mom as I did, I believe one of the first things she did when she got to heaven was to convince God to send the right woman into my life to be my wife. I also believe my mom may have met with some angels shortly after her arrival in heaven, because I met Kim three weeks after Mom died. Although Kim wasn't a Christian then, she is more responsible than anyone else for my relationship with the Lord. I knew enough to be sure that I wanted a Christian wife, and I knew that if Kim was going to believe, *I* had better get right. Kim got fired up about Christ, and I had to work just to stay a step ahead.

And you know what I discovered? I discovered just how great our Savior is by studying and praying to stay ahead of my newly believing wife.

Soon we had two awesome sons, and I grew even closer to the Lord through my prayers for them. Every day was a new adventure in my relationship with God, and the more I served Him, the more I loved Him. I switched careers because of a conviction that the Lord needed Christian teachers in the public schools. I coached football and track and got to pray with boys I coached who were in the same place I had been. *Thank You, Lord, for giving me the ultimate fun experience—the one I wasted my youth looking for.*

That day on that mountain, as my sweaty hair became matted with ice and I sat there waiting for Bob, I felt an unbelievable peace. I knew Kim and the boys would ache but that they would find comfort and strength in our God. How would the Lord use my death? I really looked forward to asking Him. I thanked Him out loud for what He had given me. It had been an awesome adventure. I promised God that I would spend that night witnessing to Bob. Bob was in for an adventure.

About that time, Bob returned. He hadn't had any success finding the way back. We started to settle in for what we both thought could be our last hours. As we positioned the snowmobiles as best we could to block the wind, we heard engines in the distance.

Bob jumped on his machine and tracked down that last crew of back-country riders, and they showed us the way out. When we pulled up to the trucks in the dark, the search-and-rescue team whom our fellow riders had called for was just heading out to look for us. We all laughed about the odds of their finding us, knowing that they were practically zero.

I could enjoy that laugh about the hopelessness of the situation I had just been in, because I realized on that mountain that I had already been found.

Pat Williams *is the head football coach and head track coach at Spring Hill High School in Spring Hill, Kansas. He is a graduate of MidAmerica Nazarene University and Baker University. Previously he was head football coach at Kemmerer, Wyoming. He and his wife, Kim, live in Spring Hill with their two sons.*

Alvin Dark

BORN TO BE A WINNER

I wasn't born just to play baseball, but it seemed that way as I was growing up. My dad played semipro ball while he worked the oilfields in Oklahoma and Louisiana. He wanted his sons to follow his footsteps onto the baseball diamond.

Some of my earliest memories are of catching for my older brother. But since my father was a second baseman, I gravitated toward focusing on shortstop. Through junior and senior high school I participated in some sport every day. In the fall it was football; during the winter it was basketball. But when the weather warmed up, I spent every possible minute on the baseball diamond. Then, when school was out for the year, I played American Legion ball all summer. I wanted to be the very best I could be. I spent every minute I could either practicing or playing baseball.

That same motivation and determination has followed me into my Christian walk. Once I became a believer, I determined to be the best Christian possible. I began to spend time in His Word and in His presence. I can tell you honestly that the joy of my life is following Jesus Christ.

During World War II I served my country as a Marine stationed in China. I didn't get to play much baseball, but I kept in shape by playing basketball for the Marines. It was around this time that my dad wrote the Boston Braves a letter about me.

In those days there was not a draft for players as we have now. But when I returned from my time with the Marines, a

Braves scout was there waiting to watch me play. When he asked me to put down the amount I would sign for, I did. I signed with the Braves right out of the Marines and began a 28-year journey that included 14 years of playing baseball and 14 years managing.

I was an untested rookie, and like all the other untested rookies, I began my career in Triple A. For me it was the AAA Milwaukee Brewers. I had to wait for my opportunity to play, but when I did I was able to help my club win the Little World Series, and I was named Minor League Rookie for that year.

The next year I moved up to the big league and played for the Braves. I was named Rookie of the Year in that league, too—quite an honor for an "oil patch kid." My baseball career was taking off, but my spiritual life wasn't developing so well. I had given my heart to the Lord when I was 11, but I had not matured in my faith.

I was privileged to play in three All-Star games and to manage two others. I played in three World Series games and managed two others. In consecutive years I managed the Oakland A's to one world championship and one division title. But those accolades did not bring me the greatest and most lasting joy in my life.

In 1971 we were living in Miami and attending a strong Bible-believing church. My wife, Jackie, and I began attending a Bible study together. We were required to study a number of chapters every week, and as I studied, I finally began to grow spiritually. We recommitted our lives to Christ and became witnessing Christians. I carried my Bible with me on the team's road trips. Finally, my spiritual development began to catch up with my baseball development.

In 1974 Charlie Findley rehired me to manage the Oakland A's. Findley had fired me twice in the same night in 1967 because I refused to suspend a player on the team. He fired me, then called back and rehired me. When I still refused to carry out his wishes, he fired me again.

Why did I go back to work for such a volatile man? Because God had a plan.

One day Whitey Spoelstra, a newspaper writer, called and asked me if I would be interested in starting chapel services for our players. He even offered to help line up speakers for us. Since Jesus was Lord of my life, I said yes.

In those days the A's organization was made up of a wild bunch of guys—unlikely Bible study candidates. Only three players showed up at the first chapel service. Two years later, though, the entire team attended regularly, as well as a number of sports writers.

Fourteen men gave their hearts to Christ. Without a doubt, those were the happiest two years of my life. During that same time period, four couples who were contemplating divorce put their marriages back together—and they're still together today.

According to the world, those men had everything: money, fame, world championships. But they found something special and lasting and truly rewarding when God took them to a greater level of living.

The most pleasant and rewarding experiences in life aren't found in world championships. I've found my greatest joy in living as I walk each day with my loving Lord and Savior.

Alvin Dark *spent 14 years playing in major league baseball. He played in three All Star games and three World Series. He is a former manager of the Oakland Athletics. He spent the first half of his life living for baseball, and the second half is being spent living for Jesus. He and his wife, Jackie, live in Easley, South Carolina. They have six children.*

Grant Teaff
A PLAN AND A PURPOSE

As the DC3s wheels touched the runway in Abilene, Texas, I felt a great sense of relief. My football team and coaching staff were safely on the ground. The previous morning an excited team and coaching staff had boarded a similar DC3 to fly to Monroe, Louisiana, to engage in a collegiate football game between McMurry College and Northeast Louisiana. In 1963 not many Division III football teams flew to their games. During my three years as head football coach at McMurry, I was able to save enough money to allow our team to fly to two games in 1963. Just 28 years old, I had been the head football coach at McMurry College for three years. I was meticulously following my elaborate plan to reach high-level goals in my chosen profession—coaching football.

Though I was too small and too slow to be an outstanding football player on the high school or collegiate level, my desire to be educated and to become a coach—like my high school coaches—motivated me to use every tool at my disposal to be the best football player I could be. My family had given me a very sound value system and work ethic, and my coaches taught me how to win on the athletic field. When I decided I wanted to coach, I was not content with just coaching—I wanted to be a successful coach on the highest level known to me at that time.

The highest level of football I knew in the early 1950s was the Southwest Conference, which was made up of the major colleges in Texas and the University of Arkansas. It had the reputation of being one of the best football conferences in America. Thus, I aspired to be a head coach in the Southwest Conference, and my success by 1963 had put me in a position of achieving that maximum goal. I was probably too naive to understand that a no-talent football player who would have to go to college as a walk-on and never play for Bear Bryant or coach for Darrell Royal had a minimal chance of becoming a head coach in the Southwest Conference. Since I had trained myself never to think in negative terms, my question was not *would* I become a head coach in the Southwest Conference but *when.*

In 1956 I met and married a beautiful Texas Tech cheerleader, Donell Phillips. She immediately latched on to my goals and became an instant helpmate. She knew and loved the game of football and recognized that I had a clearly defined goal in the area of my profession.

As a 12-year-old in Snyder, Texas, I had accepted Christ as my personal Savior. Like many kids that age, I didn't understand fully what I had done; however, I knew inside that I had done the right thing. I freely admit that through my high school and college careers I did not spend my time leading campus religious organizations. I spent my time preparing to be a head coach in the Southwest Conference. I wasn't a bad person—it's just that my faith was not a major priority for me. As I look back now, it appears to me that God clearly had a plan for me.

My wife and I made a vital decision early on in our marriage to follow Christ. Here I was, a 22-year-old man filled with a zeal to succeed, with a 20-year-old woman who was committed to helping me succeed, sitting at a little kitchen table in a $75-a-month apartment on Baylor Street in Lubbock, Texas, committing to having Jesus Christ as the foundation of our marriage and further committing that any children brought into our family would be raised within a Christian environment, church, and Christ-centered home.

We moved from Lubbock to Abilene, where I took a job as the head track coach and assistant football coach to begin reaching my ultimate goal professionally and set in motion the spiritual goals that Donell and I had set. I became the youngest deacon chairman in the history of our church. Donell was the church pianist, and we both taught Sunday School. Every time the doors opened at that church, we were there, and as our three little girls came along, they were there as well. We both knew the Bible backward and forward, and I could preach a sermon with the best of the young preachers. Within three years I had become the youngest college head football coach in America at McMurry College. We were on our way.

Fast-forward to Saturday, September 28, 1963. Our coaches and team landed in Monroe, Louisiana, enjoyed a pregame meal at a restaurant, and then went to the stadium to play the game. I should have known this was not going to be a normal evening. The game ended on a questionable play that allowed Northeast Louisiana to win in the last second of play. Furious with the loss and what I perceived to be very poor officiating, we boarded the plane for the flight back to Abilene, Texas.

The pilots and stewardess arrived in a taxicab, obviously late. They hurried onto the plane, closed the doors, and fired the engines. The plane was in a position on the runway where we did not have to taxi. With the engines revved up, we moved down the runway. Seated in a front seat and looking out a window on the left, I soon realized that we were just barely off the ground yet were dangerously close to the pine trees at the end of the runway. The engines strained as the plane turned sharply to the left and swung around to make an emergency landing. Something was wrong. In the haste of getting onto the plane and not having to taxi, the pilots had unfortunately left the elevator locked at the tail of the airplane. An airplane is not supposed to fly with the elevators locked.

There was incredible tension in the cabin as we realized that the pilots were struggling to get us down safely. Their inability to feather the flaps left us too far off the runway when they decreased the power in the engine for landing. The DC3 dropped dramatically, hit the runway, and bounced into the air. It felt as though we were going to go wingtip over wingtip. The year before, a DC3 carrying a football team from Cal Poly in San Luis Obispo, California, had crashed and killed some players and coaches. It flashed through my mind that we were in for the same fate. Miraculously, the pilots gained control of the plane, shot the power to the two engines, and we remained airborne. They circled the city again and came in for the second attempted landing.

That time they took a much lower angle and were able to touch down; however, the left landing gear had been destroyed in the first aborted landing, and we were on one wheel. The left side of the plane dropped. The prop started hitting the asphalt, and sparks began flying. The pilots realized that we were going to crash, so they pulled the nose of the plane up, shot the power to the engines again, and we are airborne once more. While we circled the city of Monroe, the cabin door opened, and the copilot stepped back to where I was seated and told me we had a problem. I *knew* we had a problem! He explained that our left landing gear had been destroyed, the electrical system was affected, and we were to fly to Shreveport, Louisiana, to a strategic air command base to crash-land the plane.

The stewardess instructed our coaches and players on proper positioning for the crash landing. The remaining lights in the passenger cabin flickered and went out. After about 15 minutes the silence in the plane was broken when one of my players called out, "Coach Teaff, will you pray for us? We're really scared."

Having learned to pray publicly early on, I could mouth a

prayer with the best of them; however, this was a different circumstance all together. Standing in the aisle, holding on to the seats on either side, bowing my head, I prayed the most fervent prayer I ever prayed in my life. Somewhere during the prayer, I said, *Surely God, You have a plan, a purpose, and a will for each life on this plane, and I pray right now that we might seek and live Your plan in the days and years ahead.* It was in many ways a selfish prayer, as I was asking for the life of our players and coaches, but somehow I was led to express the challenge that we all faced if we lived, and that was to seek God's plan for our lives.

I sat down and began to think about my own life, which could be rapidly coming to an end. As a coach should, I began to evaluate each phase of my life and found myself woefully lacking. Although successful and ahead of my personal plan for becoming a Southwest Conference head coach, I found myself falling short as a husband, father, leader, and particularly as a follower of Christ. I silently asked God to forgive me and to give me a clearer understanding of His plan for my life. Scriptures began to flash through my mind that I had learned and quoted many times. "I am come that [you] might have life, and . . . have it more abundantly" (John 10:10, KJV). "We know that all things work together for good to them that love God, to them who are the called according to his purpose" (Rom. 8:28, KJV). And finally, the words from Jeremiah kept blinking in my mind like a neon sign: "'I know the plans I have for you,' declares the LORD, 'plans to prosper you and not to harm you, plans to give you hope and a future'" (Jer. 29:11).

About that time the pilot's voice came over the intercom, and he said, "Brace yourselves—we're going in," I looked out the window and could see the runway ten or so feet below me when the pilot shut the engines down. The plane dropped, struck the runway with the fuselage, and simultaneously the left engine prop dug into the runway. Sparks flew everywhere. I heard an explosion, and the right engine blazed. With the sparks from the fuselage and the burning engine, it was as bright as day inside the plane. The plane came to a stop. Two of the coaches kicked open the back door, unloaded the stewardess and the players, then the pilots, and we all stood back away from the plane as it continued to burn. There was not a scratch on a single player, coach, or member of the crew. We had all miraculously survived. I called everyone together, we put our arms around each other, and I prayed a prayer of thanksgiving. Isn't it interesting that our prayers of thanksgiving are never quite as fervent as our prayers of asking?

After a sleepless night, the players and coaches on Sunday morning loaded onto a plane that had been flown in from Fort Worth, Texas, to pick us up. One of my players, who no longer trusted the pilots or the plane, retrieved his playing helmet from the wreckage and wore it as the plane took off for Abilene.

Three hours later, the plane came to a stop on the tarmac in Abilene, Texas, and a fortunate group of players and coaches unloaded to the well-wishing of hundreds of friends and family members. Donell and my two little girls, Tammy and Tracy, were waiting for me at the steps of the plane. Never had hugs or kisses from my loved ones meant more or felt better. As I was ushered away to a press conference, I yelled to Donell that I would meet her at church in a couple of hours.

The media pointed out that we had literally survived four opportunities to die in one night and asked for my reaction. I honestly don't remember what I said to the media, because my thoughts were on what I said to God during my prayer the night before. After the press conference, I drove across Abilene to our church. The service had started, and as I walked down the aisle looking for Donell and the girls, I heard my pastor's voice. Earl Sherman was talking about the churches in the city of Abilene offering prayers that morning thanking God for our deliverance.

Just as I started to sit down by Donell and the girls, the pastor said, "Surely God has a plan, a purpose, and a will for every individual on that plane." His words stopped me in my tracks. Overcome with emotion, I turned and walked out the back of the church and started to run as hard as I could. I couldn't help it—I had to get to the McMurry football field house, a small concrete block building that housed the dressing room for the players and coaches. I rushed into the players' dressing room, where each locker displayed the individual player's name. Kneeling before each locker and calling out the player's name, I thanked God for my team members' lives and asked Him to show the players the plan He had for them. I did the same thing in the coaches' dressing room, and then I walked into the training room and knelt down beside a training table. My simple prayer was *God, I commit my life to You totally. I'll go where You want me to go, do what You want me to do. If You want me to go to the seminary, I'll go; if You want me to go to the mission field, I'll go; but God, You know from early childhood that I felt coaching is where I should be. And if You can use me as a coach, I'll use my talents and abilities to serve You while serving others.*

I thank God that His plan was to leave me in the coaching profession, and for 32 years while reaching my personal goals, I worked hard to serve Him to the best of my ability. I believe that God called me to the coaching profession, which proves He can use us wherever we are. In 1993 He called me to a new opportunity when the American Football Coaches Association asked me to serve as their executive director. How great it is to realize that God's plan does not end when we change jobs or reach a certain age! He prepared me my entire lifetime for my current responsibilities. God has a plan and a purpose for each one of us, and our job is to seek that plan.

Find God's plan for your life. Then, as with me, you'll find incredible joy in letting Him direct your life.

Grant Teaff *is executive director of the American Football Coaches Association. He served as head coach at McMurry College and Angelo State University before becoming head football coach at Baylor University, where he led the team for 21 years.* College Sports Magazine *ranked him as one of the ten most influential administrators in college athletics. Grant and his wife, Donell, live in Waco, Texas.*